# DONNA WILLSON

スコットランドからやってきた、
ニットの人形とテキスタイル

ODD OBJECTS & TEXTILES

ODD OBJECTS & TEXTILES
DONNA WILSON

Published in 2013 by BNN, Inc.
1-20-6, Ebisu-minami, Shibuya-ku,
Tokyo, 150-0022, Japan
world_info@bnn.co.jp
www.bnn.co.jp/EG/


ISBN978-4-86100-900-6
Printed in Japan

# DONNA WILSON

こんにちは、私はドナ・ウィルソンです。もう私の作品をご存知の方もいるでしょうし、この本を手に取って初めて目にされる方もいるでしょう。私はロンドンの東部にあるスタジオで、テキスタイルのデザインと、どこかおかしなオブジェや人形を作っています。みんなが見て笑顔になれるような柄や色彩が大好きです。テキスタイルやこんな人形を作りながら暮らすことができるなんて、始めた頃は思ってもみませんでした。

私はスコットランドの北東にある小さな町の、思いやりのある家族の中で育ちました。私の祖母は、バイタリティのある人でした。たくさんの人の手助けをしたり、誰にでも話し掛けたり、また自分の心に耳を傾けているようなとてもユニークな人でした。その時代には珍しく、祖母は若い頃にアメリカに旅行をしたこともあるんです。彼女はいつも私に絵を描いたり、クリエイティブになるように勧めてくれました。母はいつも私にやりたいことをやりなさいと教えてくれました。彼女は色のセンスがあったので、私はそれを受け継いだのかもしれません。父にはビジネスのセンスがありました。彼の農園はとても成功していたんですよ。

アートは私のただひとつ得意な科目だったので、当然のようにアート系の大学に進学しました。そこでテキスタイルを専攻しました。糸を使って布を編み、柄、色、手触りなどを、一から自分の手で作ることができるこの科目は、私にとって魅力的でした。それがあっという間に完成するのを見るのも楽しいものです。

Hi, I am Donna Wilson. Nice to meet you! Some of you may already know my work, and to some it might be new and you are seeing it here for the first time. I am a textile designer and also make some odd objects and creatures in my studio in east London. I love pattern, colour, and things that make you smile. This year is a very special year for me as it marks my 10 year anniversary. I never would have imagined in my wildest dreams that I would be making weird creatures for a living!

I grew up in rural northeast Scotland. I am very lucky to have come from a very caring family — my grandma was such an inspiring character. She would help so many people and always speak to everyone she met. She was unique as she seemed to follow her heart and even travelled to the USA when she was quite young, which was unheard of in those days. She was always very encouraging and inspired me to pick up some paints and be creative. My mum always taught me to do what I want to do. She has a very good eye for colour, so I hope that I inherited that. My dad has a very good business sense, which comes with being a successful farmer in Scotland.

英国王立美術大学で学んでいた2003年からニットの人形を作り始め、卒業してすぐに自分の会社を立ち上げました。お金をかき集めて、すべてのニットを自分で作れるように家庭用の編み機を買いました（今でも当時と同じ編み機を使っています）。それが私の人生を変えたのです！ スピーディーに商品が作れるようになって、世界中の可愛らしいお店で売ってもらえるようになりました。

私の仕事で一番楽しいことは、新しい商品をデザインすること。10年経った今だって、新しいサンプルが仕上がる時はワクワクしています！ 打ち合わせやメールにたくさんの時間が割かれてしまいますが、実際に手を動かして作る時が私にとって何よりも楽しい時間。それから、ペインティングやスケッチも大好き。いつだって頭のクリエイティブな部分を動かすように心掛けています。

会社が大きくなった今では、自分の手ですべての商品を作ることはできませんが、イギリスの国内生産、ハンドメイドのクオリティは変わりません。イングランドとスコットランドの国境近くにある工場には長くお世話になっています。夫婦経営の小さな工場なのですが、私のスタジオで編めないニットを請け負ってくれています。陶器はイギリスで「陶器の里」と呼ばれるストーク＝オン＝トレントの小さな工場にお願いしていて、イギリスのクラフトマンシップを絶やさないようにしています。

この10年という節目に出版するこの本で、私の作品や世界を見ていただけたら光栄です。人形、陶器、テキスタイル、そしてたくさんの柄と色彩。それから、インスピレーションやスケッチ……！ 私のカラフルな世界へようこそ。心を込めてひとつひとつの作品を作るその過程を、一緒に楽しんでください。

Art was the only subject that I was good at in school. And so that naturally progressed into attending art college. I think I chose textiles because it was very hands-on and I liked the process of printing and creating something from scratch. Knitting still amazes me — I love the fact that you can create a fabric from a single strand of yarn and have complete control over the pattern, colour and texture. It's also so instant you can see it grow.

I started making odd knitted creatures while I was studying at the Royal College of Art. In 2003, I graduated and I set up my company straight away. Everything was made by me on a domestic knitting machine, which are the same machines as I use now. I remember when I got enough money to buy a motor for that machine, and my life completely changed!! I was able to make things a lot faster. I did a few small shows and began selling my work to some lovely shops around the world.

The most enjoyable part of my job is designing new products, and I still get really excited when I see new samples for the first time! A lot of my time is taken up with organizing and sending emails, so it's a joy to do something hands on and practical. I also love painting and sketching too, and feel like I always have to exercise the creative side of my brain.

As the company has grown, and it's not just me who makes everything anymore, it was really important that I maintain the hand made quality, and keep all the production done within the UK. So we have worked with the same supplier who is based in the Scottish borders. It' a small husband and wife team, and they work very hard to get all our knitting done. Our ceramics are made in a small factory in Stoke on Trent too, so we try to keep British craftsmanship alive.

In this book, I wanted to show all sides of my work, from creatures to ceramics, and textiles with a lot of pattern and colour and a little bit of inspiration and sketches. So I hope you enjoy this snap shot into my colourful world and how we make things one by one, with a lot of care, attention, and love.

TABLE OF CONTENTS

# ニットの人形

# CREATURES

私の一番最初の作品は、ニットの人形。インスピレーションの源は子どもたちの描く絵です。子どもたちのピュアな想像力を借りて、風変わりだけど、どこか愛嬌のあるキャラクターを作っています。

最初の頃は、人形が出来上がったら、私はいろんな人に見せて、それぞれのキャラクターの好きなこと、嫌いなこと、特徴などを話してまわりました。そうすることで、みんなが人形と関係性を築き、愛着を持てるようになる、そして人形たちを新しい友達として迎えてくれるようになると思ったんです。

初めはすべて自分で手作りしていました。家に編み機があったので、パターンを編んで、それを縫い合わせて…。忙しい時には、大きなバッグに作りかけの人形を詰め込んで、バスの中で目を刺繍をすることもありました。きっとバスに乗り合わせていた人は、おかしな人形を縫っている私を見て不思議に思ったでしょう。でも、私はそんなこと気にもしませんでした。ともかく、人形を仕上げることに夢中でしたから！

毎年、私は新しい人形をいくつか発表しているので、その代わりにいくつかの古い人形を作るのを諦めなくてはなりません。新しい友達が増えた喜びと同時に、愛着のある友達と別れなくてはならないのは、私にとっても辛いことです。人形のこととなると、どうしても感傷的になってしまいます。やっぱり、これが私の原点ですから。

My knitted creatures were the first thing I made and were inspired by children's drawings, because I love the way that children draw. I wanted to capture this innocent naivety in my creatures and make an odd but not too scary character.

I started to give each one a tag telling people what they liked and disliked, and a little bit about them. I felt this was a way of getting people to relate to the creatures, and love them and then give them a nice home, as if they were adopting a new friend. In the beginning I used to make them all myself. I had a knitting machine in my room at home, and I would knit the pattern, then sew the bodies, and sometimes if I was really busy I would take a big bag of half made creatures on the bus with me to sew their eyes on. People must have seen me sitting on the bus with funny creatures sewing faces on them, but I didn't mind, I just had to get them done!

Each year I try to design some new ones, but it's always difficult to discontinue some of the old ones. I think I will always have a soft spot for the creatures, as they are what I started with.

## PEEPING TOM

Hi, I'm PEEPING TOM. I'm inquisitive and like telling jokes. I dislike smelly feet. I have a big, yellow, friendly face. I like sticking my nose into thing.

こんにちは、ピーピング・トムです。僕は知りたがりで、冗談を言うのが好き。足が臭いのは嫌いだよ。大きな黄色い顔が特徴で、何にでも鼻を突っ込むのが好き。

# WOLFIE

こんにちは、ウルフィーです。僕はシャイで、はにかみ屋さんなの。ちょっと変わりもので、ナイーブな心を持ってるんだ。

Hi, I'm WOLFIE. I'm shy and bashful, and like collecting spoons. A little bit of an eccentric, I am a kind chap who has a sensitive side.

# BRUCE MONKEY

こんにちは、ブルース・モンキーです。僕は詩を書くことと、台所でいろいろな実験をするのが好き。でも片付けは嫌い。ジムで体を鍛えて、健康管理をおこたりません。

Hi, I'm BRUCE MONKEY. I like writing poetry and experimenting in the kitchen. I dislike cleaning up. I work out at the gym and like to look after myself.

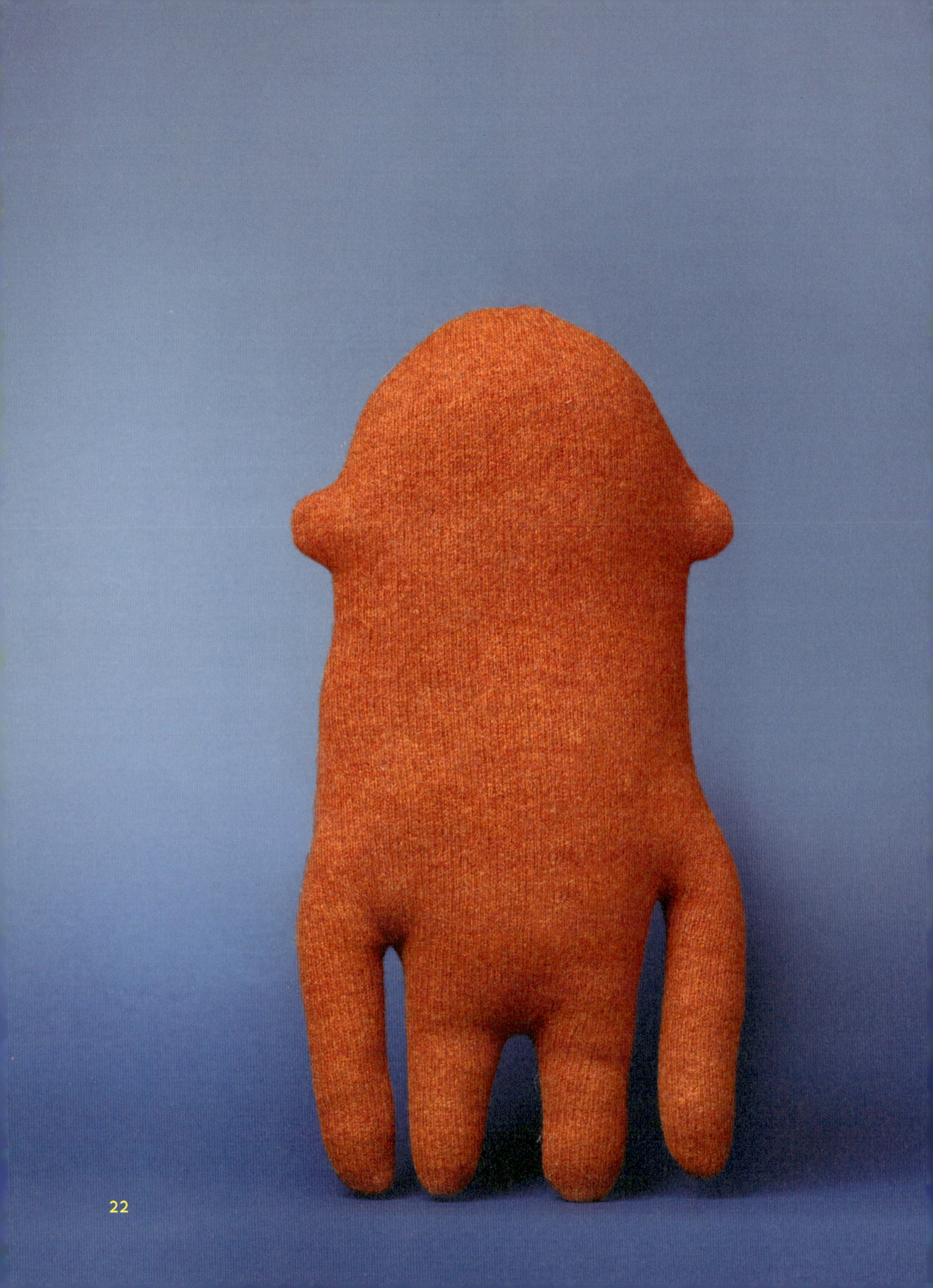

## NEEP

こんにちは、ニープです。僕は風船を膨らますのが好き。それから、いつも愛を探している。「ニープ」はスコットランド語で、“カブ”や“スェーデンカブ”って意味なんだ。

Hi, I'm NEEP. I like blowing bubbles and I'm also looking for love...Neep means turnip, or swede in Scottish.

## JASPER

こんにちは、ジャスパーです。僕は物語を話すのが好き。それから、暗いところでものを見るのが得意。小柄で、穏やかな声で話します。僕は野菜の仲間だから、とってもヘルシーですよ。

Hi, I'm JASPER. I like telling stories and can see in the dark. I am a small, soft spoken character, I am part of the vegetable range so I'm very healthy.

## BILLY BROCOLLI

こんにちは、ビリー・ブロッコリーです。僕はヒップホップが好きで、ミックステープを作るのが趣味。90年代のキッズみたいにフラットトップのヘアスタイルをしてるんだ。カッコいいでしょ？

Hi, I'm BILLY BROCOLLI. I like hip hop music and making mix tapes. I have a 'flat top '90's hair cut! I am very cool, huh?

## SUKI

こんにちは、スキです。オペラとスコットランドのウイスキーが好き。私の名前の由来になったドナの日本の友達も、オペラとスコットランドのウイスキーが好きなんだって。

Hi, I'm SUKI. I love opera and Scottish whisky. I am named after a very good Japanese friend of Donna, who also loves opera and Scottish whiskey.

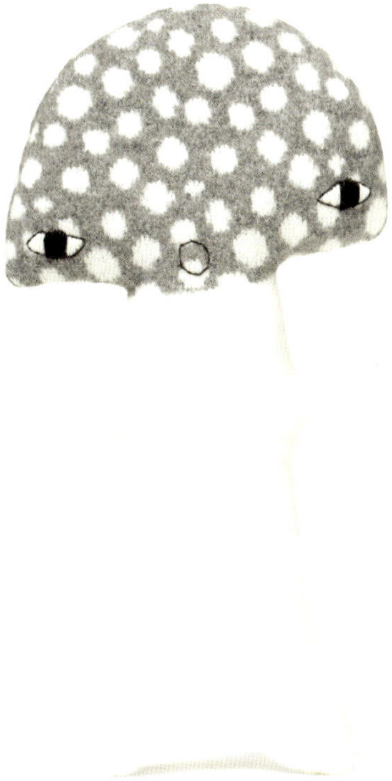

## PABLO

こんにちは、パブロです。僕はブギー・ボードが好き。だけど、日焼けでできる線が嫌い。おしゃれで、カッコいいズボンを履いていて、休暇に出かけるのが大好きなんだ。

Hi I'm PABLO. I like boogie-boarding and dislike tan lines. I am a very fashionable bear, and I have very nice trousers and love going on holiday.

## PEANUT

こんにちは、ピーナッツです。私は殻の中から出てくるのに時間がかかるんです。ドナのお姉さんのおなかに赤ちゃんがいる時に、そのおなかをピーナッツと呼んでいたことがきっかけで私が誕生したそうです。赤ちゃんがいる女の人がいたら、ぜひ私をお供にしてください。

Hi I'm PEANUT. I take a while to come out of my shell. I am named after the pregnant bump of Donna's sister, nicknamed the baby Peanut, but when he was born, they called him Fearghal. I hope other people will have me for their baby bumps!

## GINGE

こんにちは、ジンジです。僕はキスとチェリーコーラが好きで、雷が嫌い。ちょっと不機嫌そうな顔がチャームポイントの猫です。

Hi, I'm GINGE. I love kisses and cherry cola. I dislike thunder and lightning. I am a funny looking cat with a little bit grumpy look!

## WILBUR

こんにちは、ウィルバーです。僕はピンクのリンゴが好き。だけどフライドポテトは嫌い。僕は小さいけど、ビック・テッドとは大の仲良し。ビック・テッドとは２人だけのいろんなヒミツを持っているんだ。

Hi, I'm WILBUR. I like pink apples and don't like French fries. Wilbur is tiny but his best friend is Big Ted, who is huge. They share secrets and stories together.

# SMOKEY

こんにちは、スモーキーです。ハーモニカをふくのが好きで、早い時間に寝るのが嫌い。時々、友達と歌を歌って、夜更かししちゃうこともあるんだ！

Hi, I'm SMOKEY. I like playing the harmonica and dislike going to bed early. Sometimes I have a sing song with my friends and we stay up all night!

# SIDNEY

こんにちは、シドニーです。キャラメルのかかったケーキとエッグアンドスプーンレース（卵をスプーンにのせて運んで競うゲーム）が好き。本物のかたつむりみたいに目が触覚の上についてるんだ。

Hi, I'm SIDNEY. I like sticky toffee pudding and egg and spoon races. My eyes are on two feelers, like a real snail.

# SHELLY

こんにちは、シェリーです。私はガーデニングや新鮮な野菜が好きで、あくせくするのが嫌い。優しい心と、居心地の良い甲羅を持ったカメです。

Hi, I'm SHELLY. I like gardening, eating fresh veg and dislike being in a rush. I'm a tortoise with a soft heart and cosy shell.

# RILL

こんにちは、リルです。シリル・スクワール - フォックスは僕のお父さんです。エネルギーに満ちあふれていて、あちこち動き回っています。イモムシや幼虫が好き。

Hi, I'm RILL. I'm Cyril Squirrel-Fox's first child. I am very lively and never stop running around. I like caterpillars and worms.

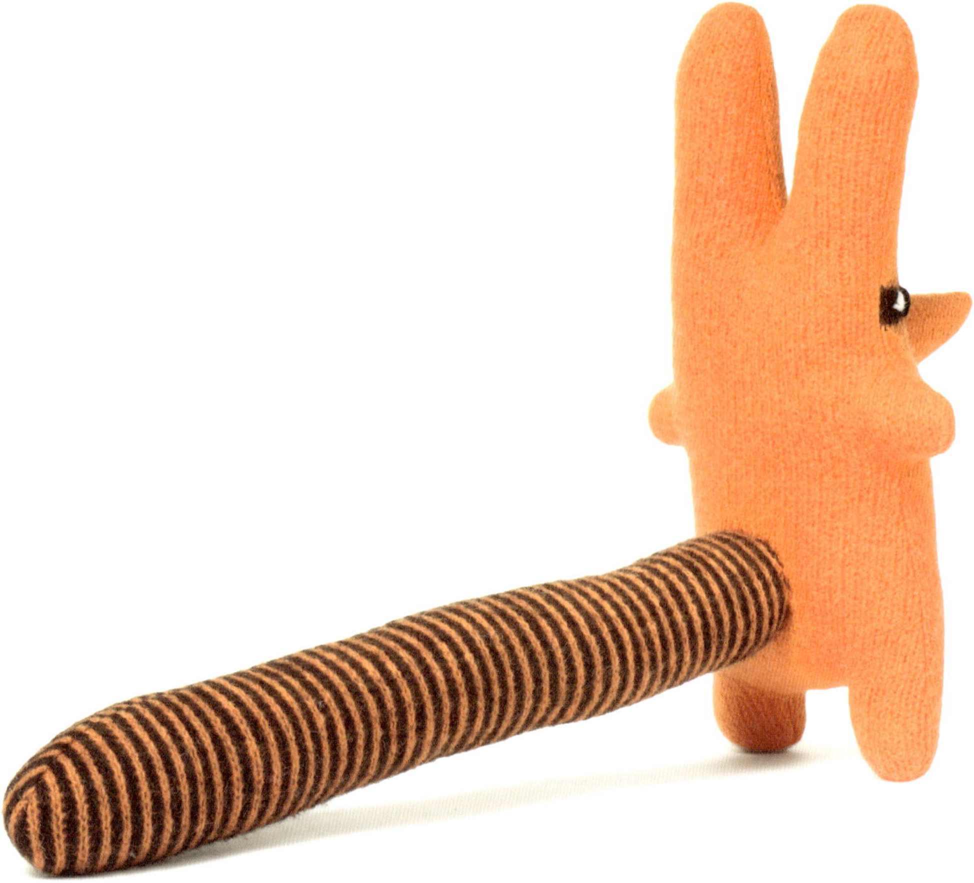

## CYRIL SQUIRREL-FOX

こんにちは、シリル・スクワール-フォックスです。僕はやんちゃ坊主。マーマレードが好きで、カッテージチーズが嫌い。イギリスのテレビ番組に出演していて、人気者なんだよ。僕のひいおじいちゃんは有名な探検家だったんだ。

Hi I'm CYRIL SQUIRREL-FOX. I am mischievous. I like marmalade and dislike cottage cheese. I am famous and have appeared on television in the uk. My great grandfather was a famous explorer.

## BIG TED

こんにちは、ビック・テッドです。チーズとピクルスのサンドウィッチが好きで、ショッピングが嫌い。僕はノッポで、いつも緑色のバンダナを首に巻いているんだ。

Hi, I'm BIG TED.
I love cheese and pickle sandwiches and dislike shopping. I am one of the biggest creatures. I always wear a green neckerchief.

## CHARLIE

こんにちは、チャーリーです。僕は目立ちたがり屋。ダンスが大好きで、雷が嫌い。僕はずっと昔にドナが教わっていた先生に似ているんだって。先生は知ってるのかな？

Hi I'm Charlie. I like to stand out in the crowd. I Love dancing and dislike thunder and lightning. I am the monkey and was named after Donna's old tutor — I wonder if he knows that.

## BIG FOX

こんにちは、ビッグ・フォックスです。僕はわんぱくで、ルールを破るのが好き。でも、小さな犬は嫌いなんだ。僕はビッグ・テッドと同じくらい背が高いんだよ。

Hi, I'm BIG FOX. I like being naughty and breaking the rules. I dislike small dogs. I'm one of the tallest creatures like Big Ted.

# ドナのある暮らし

# LIFE WITH DONNA

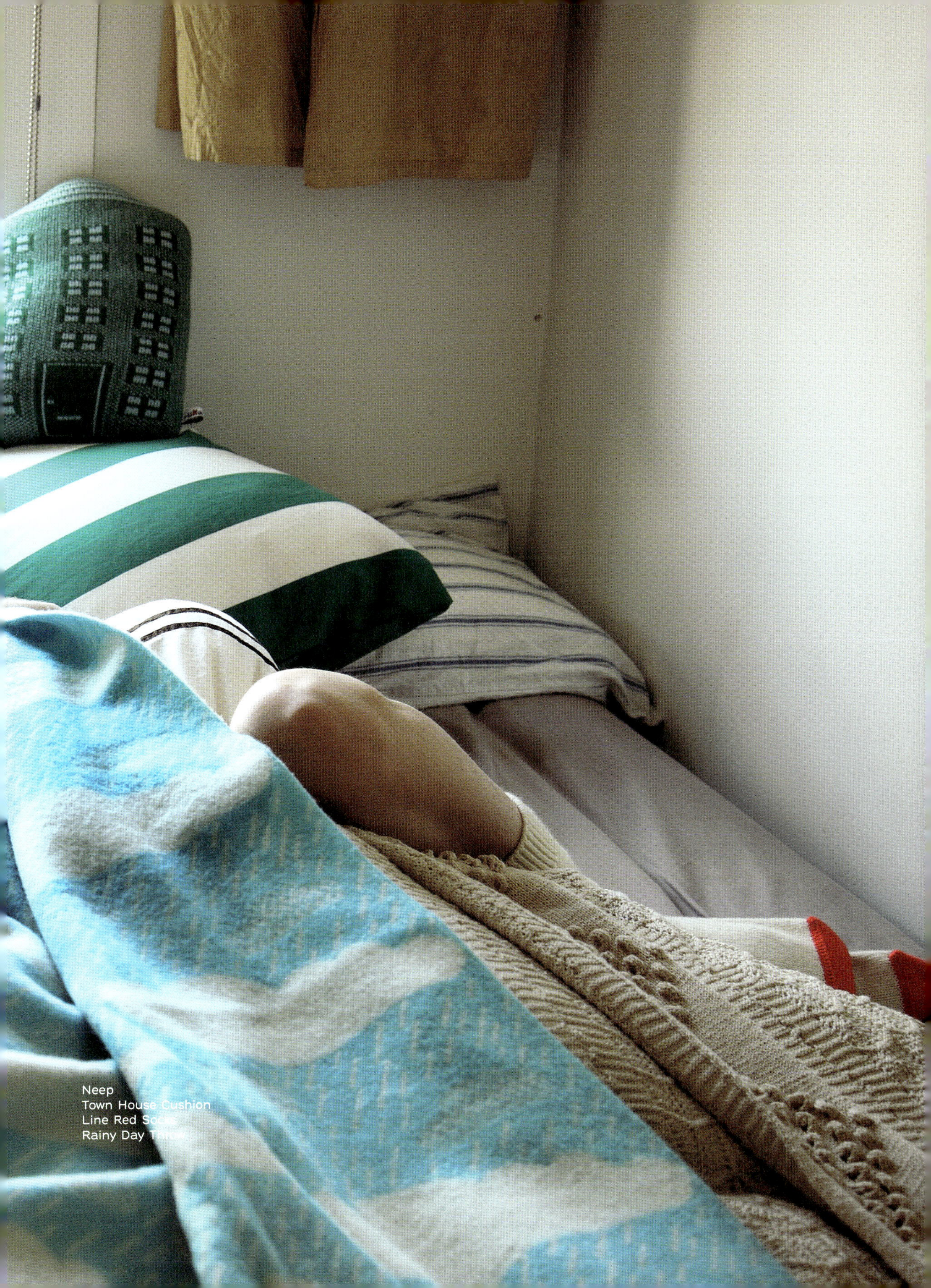

Neep
Town House Cushion
Line Red Socks
Rainy Day Throw

Billy Broccoli
Mono Cat
Wilbur
Peanut
Cupcake
Neep

Mono Cat

Terry & Tina Twin
Ziggy Pine Tree
Charlie Monkey
Baby Blue
Sidney
Pie Chart Patchwork

Log Cushion

Giant Grey Wolf

Owl Plate
Grace Plate
Fox Plate and Birdy Egg Cup
Baby Bear (Small) Bowl and
Burt Egg Cup

Fox Plate
Birdy Nest Egg Cup
Mog Plate
Birdy Walk Dinner Plate
Daddy Bear (Large) Bowl
Baby Bear (Small) Bowl
Grace Plate

Oak & Acorn Dinner Plate
Beardy Bob Plate
Burt Egg Cup
Grace Plate
Acron Small Bowl
Birdy Walk Dinner Plate

Jasper

Peeping Tom
Ginge Cat
Bruce Monkey
Cyril Squrrel-Fox
Pie Chart Patchwork

Knutsson • Holmberg-Thor
Pelle Svanslös och hans

Frank Pouffe in Zig Zag by Donna
Wilson for SCP
Dash Dot Socks
Blah Blah Mini Blanket

Frank Pouffe in Zig Zag by Donna
Wilson for SCP
Ernest Pouffe in Zig Zag by Donna
Wilson for SCP
Ernest Pouffe in Treecloud Blue by
Donna Wilson for SCP
Henry Pouffe in Zig Zag by Donna
Wilson for SCP
Mountain Spot Rug by Donna Wilson
for SCP

Baby Blue

Caterpillar Scarf
Circus Hat

BLACK EYEWEAR
BLACK
BLACK
BLACKEYEWEAR.COM
020 7637 2144

Wilbur

House Scarf

SONY

Mono Cat

Fir Tree
Neep
Wolfie
Peeping Tom
Stripey Head
Sidney
Rainy Day Mini Blanket

Rainy Day Mini Blanket
Charlie Monkey
Hand knitted Cyril Squirrel fox

Clyde Scarf
Scandi Hat
Fir Tree (Small)
Puddleman
Mountain spot rug by Donna Wilson
for SCP

Neep
Sunshine Cushion
Bader Cushion
Fir Tree (Small)
Scope rug by by Donna Wilson for SCP
Circus Arm Warmers
(Worn as Leg Warmers)

Swan Scarf (Big)
Bunny Scarf

Scandi Scarf
Scandi Hat

Tutti Snood
Tip Top Hat

Giant Red Fox

Models: Rosalie Wagner, Frances Wall Lacey, Konrad Lindholm, Luna Paris Pina Liv Suzuki Ståhl, Sateen Panagiotopoulou, Robert Roope, Tokyo Ellery, Jack Spencer, Remy Williams + friend, Darren Hanson, Mikako Umeda, Donna Wilson

# テキスタイル

# T
# E
# X
# TILES

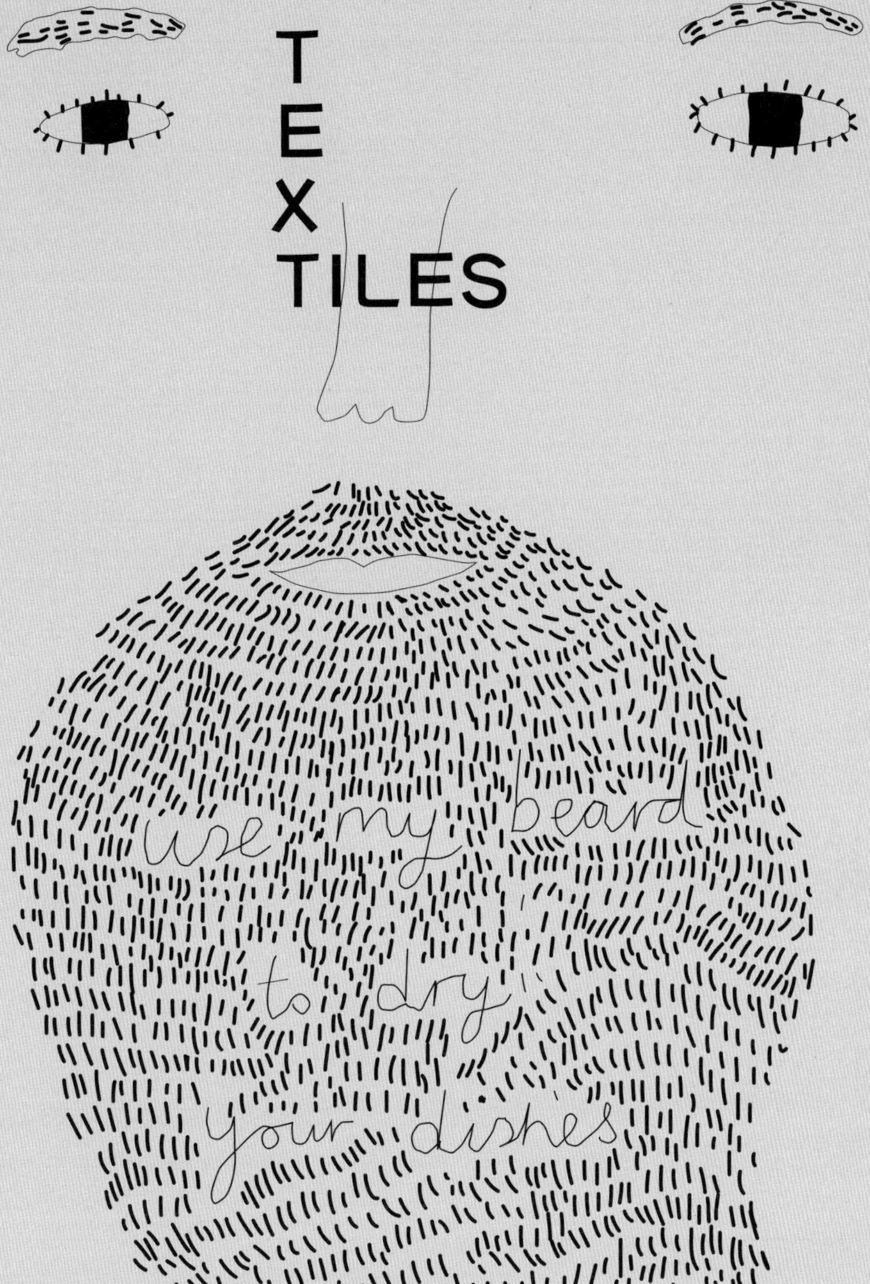

## ウール

私はいつも天然のより糸を使います。その多くはラムウールです。色が好きだし、フェルトの独特な質感も好き。それは、私が農園で育ったからかもしれません。私は子どもの頃に、羊のペットを飼っていたんです。名前は「ブラック・シープ」。彼女はいつだって私の後をついてまわっていました。さまざまなものに利用できるところもウールの魅力です。それに、暖かくもしてくれるし、涼しくもしてくれる。美しいし、柔らかいし。私は普段、30色のラムウールを使っているのですが、それらを変わった組み合わせで楽しむのが好き。それが、私らしさになっているんじゃないかな。

## WOOL

I always work with natural yarns, mainly lambswool, and I love the colours you can get as well as its felting properties.
I think it might be because I was brought up on a farm, and had a pet sheep called 'blacksheep'. She used to follow me everywhere! But I think wool is such a versatile material. It can keep you warm and keep you cool, and it's so lovely and soft. We normally use around 30 different colours of lambswool, and I enjoy using odd colour combinations. I think this variety of colour is sometimes what makes my designs different.

羊は可愛い動物です。ロンドンの家でもペットとして飼いたくなってしまうほど！

Sheep are lovely animals. I would love to have a pet sheep in my garden in London!

イギリスの家具メーカー、アーコールとのコラボレーションで作った椅子。背もたれにカラフルな毛糸を巻き付けて、特別な一脚に仕上げました。

We have done a few projects work with Ercol, an English furniture maker, where I wrapped lots of coloured yarn around the backs. It makes them really special pieces from my competitors. It's always nice to be different!

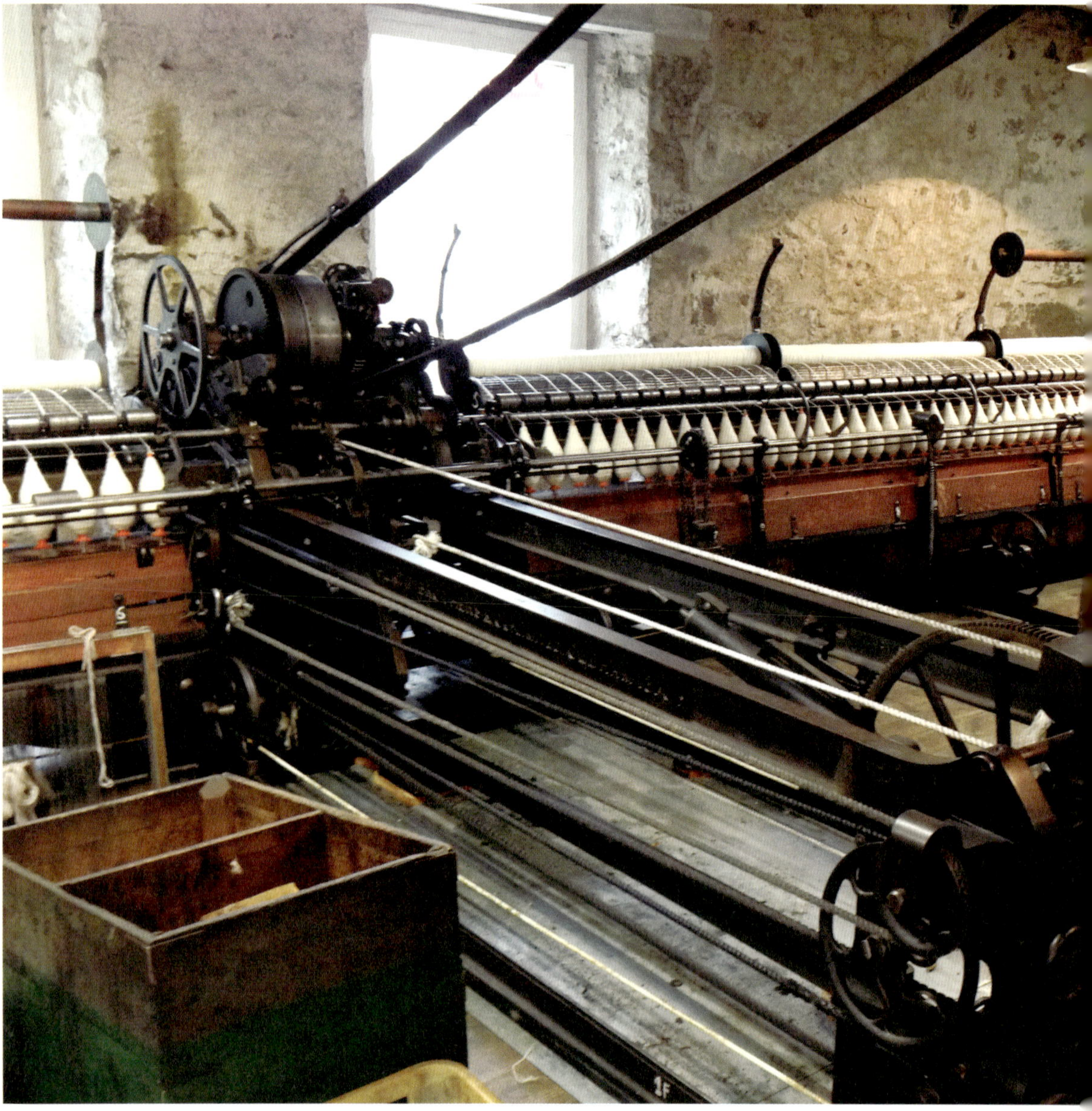

工場を見学するのは大好きです。原料が作られる工程は、いつ見ても感心してしまいます。これは、最近私が訪れたスコットランドの羊毛糸工場です。仕入れた羊の毛は、染料を調合し、毛並みを整えることで、編み物や織物をするための柔らかく美しいウールに紡がれます。ここで使われている機械はとても古く、ビクトリア時代のものだとか。まだ動いているんですよ。

スコットランドのノッカンドゥ羊毛糸工場で使われている古い紡績機。

This is an old machine for Spinning wool at Scottish mill Knockando.

I love visiting factories and I am always amazed and inspired by seeing how things are made. This is a spinning factory I visited recently near my home town in Scotland. They buy in sheep's wool and it goes through many processes to mix the colours and brush out the fibres so that it can be spun into beautiful, soft wool for knitting or weaving. The machinery they use is so old. It was made in Victorian times, but it still works really well.

## デザイン

デザインは、ノートにスケッチすることから始まります。いつどこでアイデアが思い浮かぶか分からないし、それを書き留めておかないと忘れてしまうので、ノートはいつも持ち歩いています。私のスケッチブックはマンガの落書きみたいで、素敵なものではありませんが、アイデアを忘れないようにするためには必需品なのです。スケッチの後は、ニットのサンプルを作るために、コンピュータで作業をします。変わったプログラムを使っているように見えるけど、その仕組みはとても簡単。編み機にかける時、1ピクセルは1ステッチ（縫い目）。だから、ステッチごとにデザインをしていきます。ニットが編まれる過程を見たり、いろんな色の組み合わせに挑戦するのは楽しい作業です。サンプルが出来上がったら、本格的なニット編み機にかけてもらうために、工場にデータを送ります。日本の島精機製作所というメーカーの編み機で、私のスタジオの編み機よりもずっと速く、よりたくさんの色を使って編むことができます。

## DESIGN PROCESS

I usually do sketches in a notebook first. I always try to have a notebook on me at all times. You never know when you might see something inspiring that gives you an idea, and I have a terrible memory, so if I don't write or do a quick sketch it may well get forgotten. My sketch books aren't very beautiful, they look like little cartoons, but as long as I have retained the idea it's not important. After sketching, the next stage is designing it on my computer so that I can knit up a sample. We use an odd programme that is very basic, but when you take it onto the knitting machine, one pixel equals one knitted stitch, so you can basically draw with stitches. The exciting thing is to see the design knitted up and trying out different colour combinations. After that, I send the design to our knitters who do a sample on their industrial machine. They use very advanced Japanese knitting machines called 'Shima Seiki' so they can knit a lot faster than we can, and with more colours.

Adobe Illustrator のプログラムで具体的な形にしていきます。スクリーンに映っているのは、「プレイ・タイム」というコレクションのクッションとブランケットのデザインです。

I work up the designs on Adobe Illustrator. The design in the picture is a design for cushions and blankets called 'play time'.

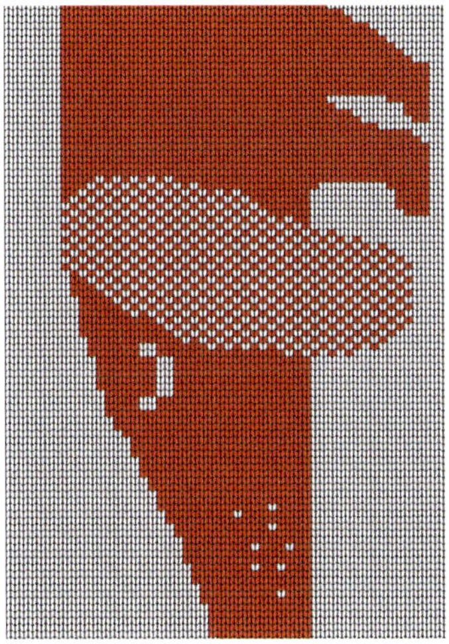

## カラー

色の組み合わせを考えるのは、楽しい作業のひとつ。日中の自然光で選ぶことが大切です。そうすれば実際にみなさんが使う時にどんな色に見えるか、どんな色の組み合わせがマッチするか分かるからです。通常は工場にカラーカードを渡して色を指定しますが、特別な色が必要な時は自分で染めることもあります。デザインにはめるとどう見えるか分からない時は、実際にサンプルを編んでみて、それを見ながら試行錯誤します。思い描く色を再現するのは難しいのですが、だからこそ出来上がった時の喜びもひとしおなのです。

## COLOUR

Choosing colour is a really fun part of my job. It's important to have natural day light so you can see the true colours and how they work with each other. We try to stick to our supplier's colour card. However, if I want something really special, we sometimes get our own colours dyed. I always find it hard to visualise a design in a certain colour until I actually knit a bit up or see a sample.
It can be difficult to get it right, but when it works, it's so satisfying.

思いもよらない組み合わせが上手くいくなんてこともあります。アイデアはマーケット、野菜、自然、人などいろいろなところから得ます。色彩は私を幸せにしてくれるんです！

Sometimes the most surprising colour combinations work the best — I get inspired by colour everywhere — the market — vegetables, the natural environment, people. Colour makes you happy!

## 編む・縫う

ニットを作る時には、まずスタジオでサンプルを作ります。工場にデザインを送る前に、自分の目で仕上がりを確かめておきたいからです。数が多いため、クッションやブランケットは工場にお願いしていますが、人形の素材となるニットは今でも私のスタジオで編んでいます。レベッカとエヴァが使い方を知っているので、編み機はほとんど一日中稼働しています。ちょっと音がうるさいので、スタジオの奥にある小さい部屋に置いています。ここで少し、私のスタジオの様子をご紹介しましょう。

## KNITTING / SEWING

We always sample designs first at the studio. I think it's important to try out the design before sending it to our knitters. The cushions and blankets are not knitted in the studio anymore, as the quantities would be too big, but we still knit the fabric for the creatures here. Rebecca and Eva can both use the domestic machines, and we have to keep the knitting machines on a lot of the day. They make a bit of a noise so it's good to have a little room to keep them in. Let me show you how we're woking in the studio.

編む — スタジオでは、ブラザーの家庭用編み機を使っています。２色しか使えないので、デザインする時はそれを念頭に置かなければいけません。編み出されたニットが絡まないように、ニットの先端におもりを付けます。編むスピードは意外と速いんですよ。

Knitting — the machine is a domestic brother machine. It can only knit two colours in one row, so you have to bear that in mind when designing. We have to put weights on the fabric so that it doesn't snag on the machine, but it still knits quite quickly.

brother
CB-1

洗う ― ウールに混ざっている油分を取り除くために洗います。スタジオでは、2台の業務用洗濯機を使っています。洗うことで、3分の2くらいに縮んで、より柔らかな肌触りに生まれ変わります。

Washing — then the wool is washed to get rid of any oils that are still in the wool. We use two commercial machines. The wool shrinks about two thirds of it's original size and it becomes a lot softer.

乾かす ― スタジオはあまり広くないので、乾かす場所を探すのが大変。でも、完全に乾くまでアイロンはかけられません。

Drying — we are always running out of room in the studio to dry things! But you can't press the knitting until it's completely dry.

アイロンをかける — スタジオには、業務用の素晴らしいアイロンがあるので、アイロン掛けは簡単でスピーディー。しっかりとシワを取って、平らにします。この工程を経て、ウールはようやく加工できる状態になります。

Ironing — we have a great industrial iron, which makes things easier and quicker. The wool all has to be pressed and any creases flattened out. The process gives the wool have a nice finish.

裁断 — ニットの端の部分を切り落とします。クッションの場合は適切なサイズに裁断。ウールは高価なものなので、切れ端を最小限にして多くの無駄を出さないように、柄を仕上がりサイズに合わせてデザインすることもあります。

Cutting — the ends have to be trimmed and cushions have to be cut down into the right shape. We try not to waste too much, as the wool is very expensive, so sometimes we have to adjust the patterns so that the waste is kept to a minimum.

縫う — 縫う前に、型紙で輪郭をなぞってから、工業用のミシンにかけます。エヴァはとても速く縫うことができます。最高の仕上がりにするために、丁寧に縫うことは大切です。ただし、時間をかけすぎると値段に影響してしまうので、それも考えながら作業を進めます。

Sewing — we use templates and draw round them before stitching around the line with an industrial sewing machine. Eva is really fast at sewing, and it's important that this is done really well so that the quality is to the highest standard. It's also important it doesn't take too long to make, as this will affect the cost.

刺繍 ― 人形とクッションは表裏逆さまにして、すべて手作業で縫っています。中にぬいぐるみ用の詰め物を入れてから、目や鼻を手で刺繍します。だから、どれひとつとして同じ形ではないんです。ちょっとずつ違うからこそ、人形に個性が出て面白い。私たちは出来上がった人形を見て、誰が縫ったのかが分かるんですよ！ それぞれに「筆跡」のようなスタイルがあるんです。

Hand embroidery — The creature or cushion normally is turned inside out and finished by hand. Each of our creatures is stuffed with toy stuffing, then the features are hand embroidered on. No two will look exactly the same. I love it that these slight variations give them more character, and normally we can tell who has made each one as each person has their own hand writing and style.

仕上げ ― 出来上がった商品は、ラベルを貼って、梱包をします。人形の場合は、それぞれの自己紹介シールを貼ります。クッションはクッションパッド、陶器はシールを貼ったきれいな箱に入れます。完成品をどうやって見せるかも大切なので、いつもシンプルで洗練されたパッケージを用意するようにしています。

Finishing — the product gets labelled and packed up, and creatures get stickers with their personalities written on them. Cushions get a cushion pad, and ceramics get a nice box with a sticker. Peresentation is important too, so we try to find nice simple packaging.

Rainy Day — Used on cushions and scarves but now only mini blankets.

雨の日 — クッション、スカーフに使用。現在ではミニブラッケットのみ。

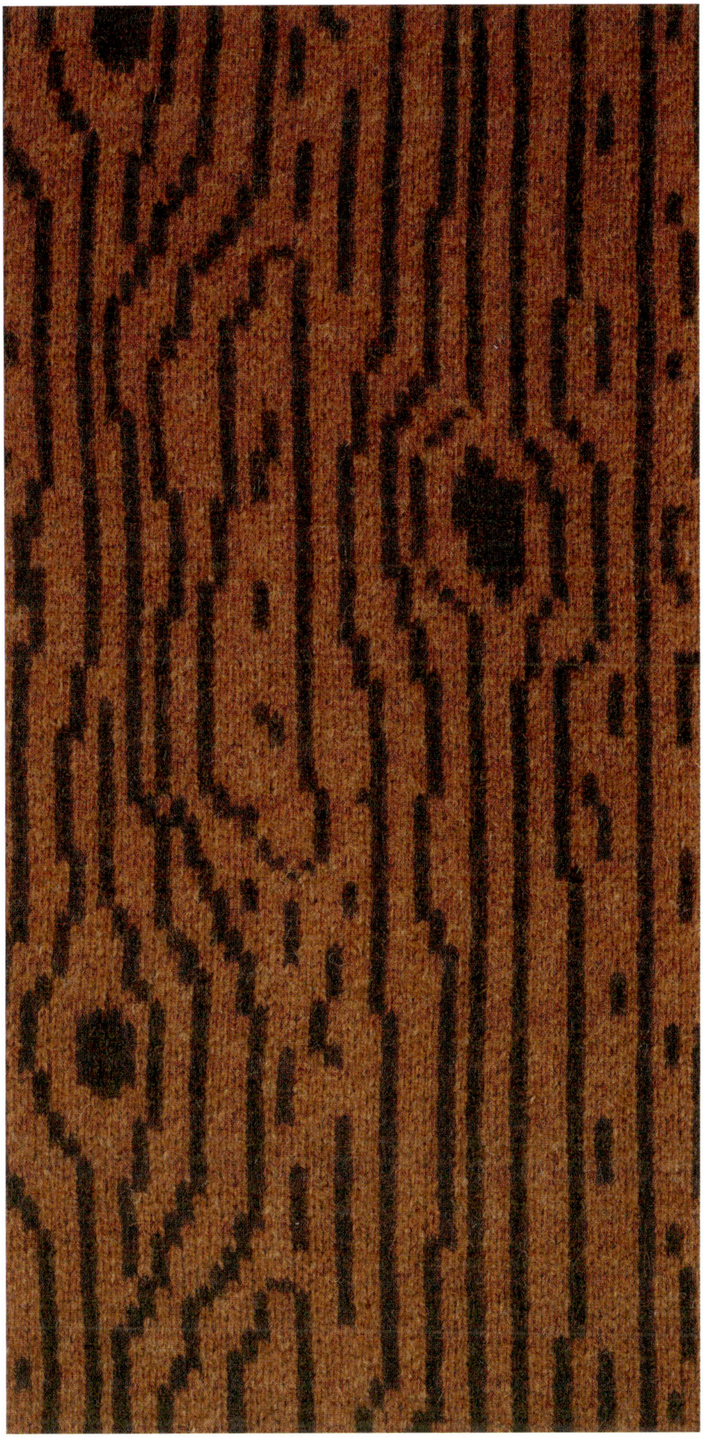

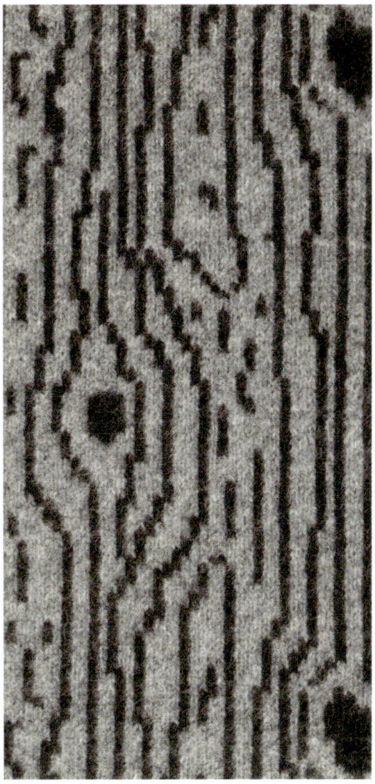

Wooly Wood — Used in cushions, big woven blankets and snoods.

ウールの木 — クッション、大きなブランケット、スヌードに使用。

Zig Zag — Made for SCP knitted pouffes.　　ジグザグ — SCP のニットプーフに使用。

Fur — Used for a fox creature's tail, a wolf creature, and the Fir Trees.

毛皮 — キツネの人形のしっぽ、オオカミの人形、もみの木のオブジェに使用。

Tutti Design — Used for snoods.　　トゥッティ・デザイン — スヌードに使用。

Graph — Used for scarves and mitts.　　グラフ ― スカーフ、ミットに使用。

Leaves and Twigs — Used for table cloths and printed cushions.

葉っぱと枝 ― テーブルクロス、プリントクッションに使用。

Ogilvy — Used for printed cushions.　　オグルヴィ — プリントクッションに使用。

Hofdi — Used in cushions and scarves.

ホフディ — クッション、スカーフに使用。

Shelley — Used for a turtle creature.　　シェリー — カメの人形に使用。

Tree Cloud — Used for SCP knitted pouffe and scarves.

木の雲 — SCP のニットプーフとスカーフに使用。

House Roof — Used for house shaped cushions.

家の屋根 — 家の形をしたクッションに使用。

Top: Log Cabin — Used for cushions, inspired by a trip to a tiny island called Fogo island, Newfoundland, Canada.

上:丸太小屋 — クッションに使用。カナダ、ニューファンドランドにあるフォーゴ島という小さな島へ旅をした時に思いついた柄。

Bottom: House of Tree — Only for sample.
下：木の家 — サンプル用。

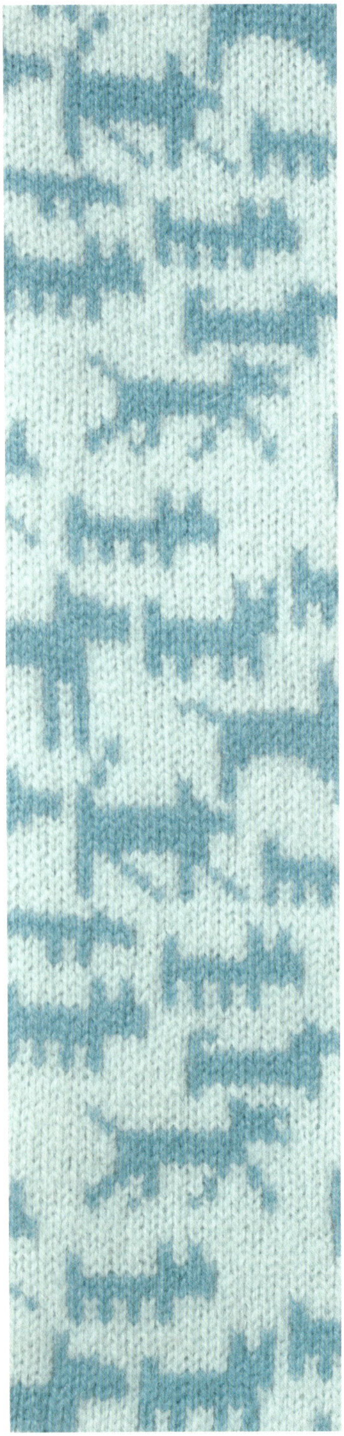

Dogs — Used on cushions and mini blankets.

犬 — クッションとミニブランケットに使用。

Fox in the Hills — Used in a cushion designed for Heal's London.

丘の上のキツネ — インテリアショップ「ヒールズ」のためにデザインしたクッションに使用。

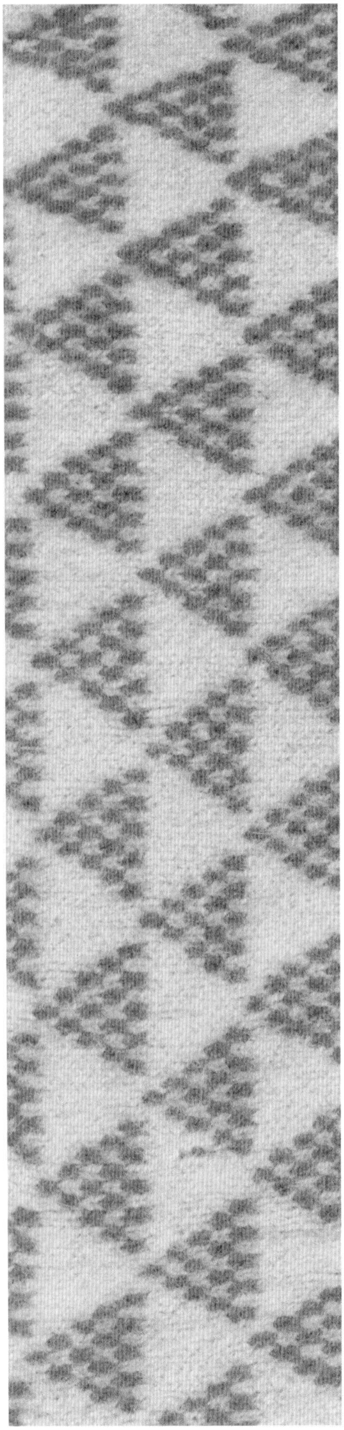

Triangles — Used on an owl creature.
三角形 — フクロウの人形に使用。

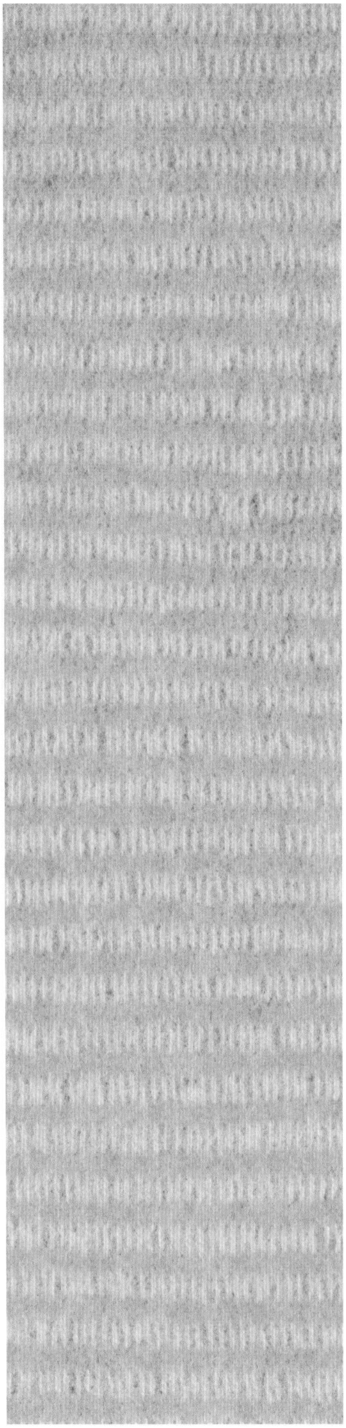

2x2 Stripe (pink) — Used for a cat creature.
2×2 ストライプ（ピンク）— 猫の人形に使用。

2x2 Stripe (black) — Used for a raccon creature's tail.
2x2 ストライプ（ブラック）— アライグマの人形のしっぽに使用。

Blah Blah — Used on cushions, scarves, mini blankets and large woven throws.

ブラ・ブラ ― クッション、スカーフ、ミニブランケット、大きな膝掛けに使用。

Circus — Used for arm warmers and hats.

サーカス — アームウォーマー、帽子に使用。

Blue Cloud — For cloud shaped cushions.

青い雲 — 雲の形をしたクッションに使用。

Spots — Originally designed for a dog creature, now used for a cat creature.

点々 — 初期は犬の人形に、現在は猫の人形に使用。

Leaf — Used for oak leaf cushions and tree hot water bottle covers.

葉っぱ — オークの葉の模様のクッション、木の模様の湯たんぽのカバーに使用。

Boat — Used on mini blankets and rectangle cushions.

ボート — ミニブランケット、長方形のクッションに使用。

Cross Detail — From House scarf.

細かい十字 — 家の模様のスカーフに使用。

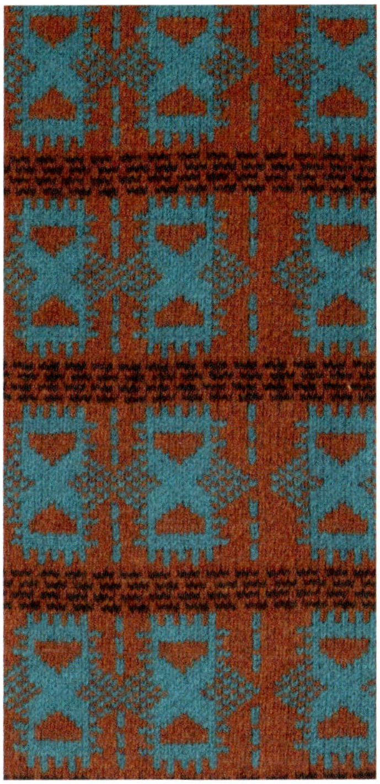

Clyde — Used on scarves.

クライド — スカーフに使用。

Small Faces — Used on mini blankets, scarves, and cushions.

小さい顔 — ミニブランケット、スカーフ、クッションに使用。

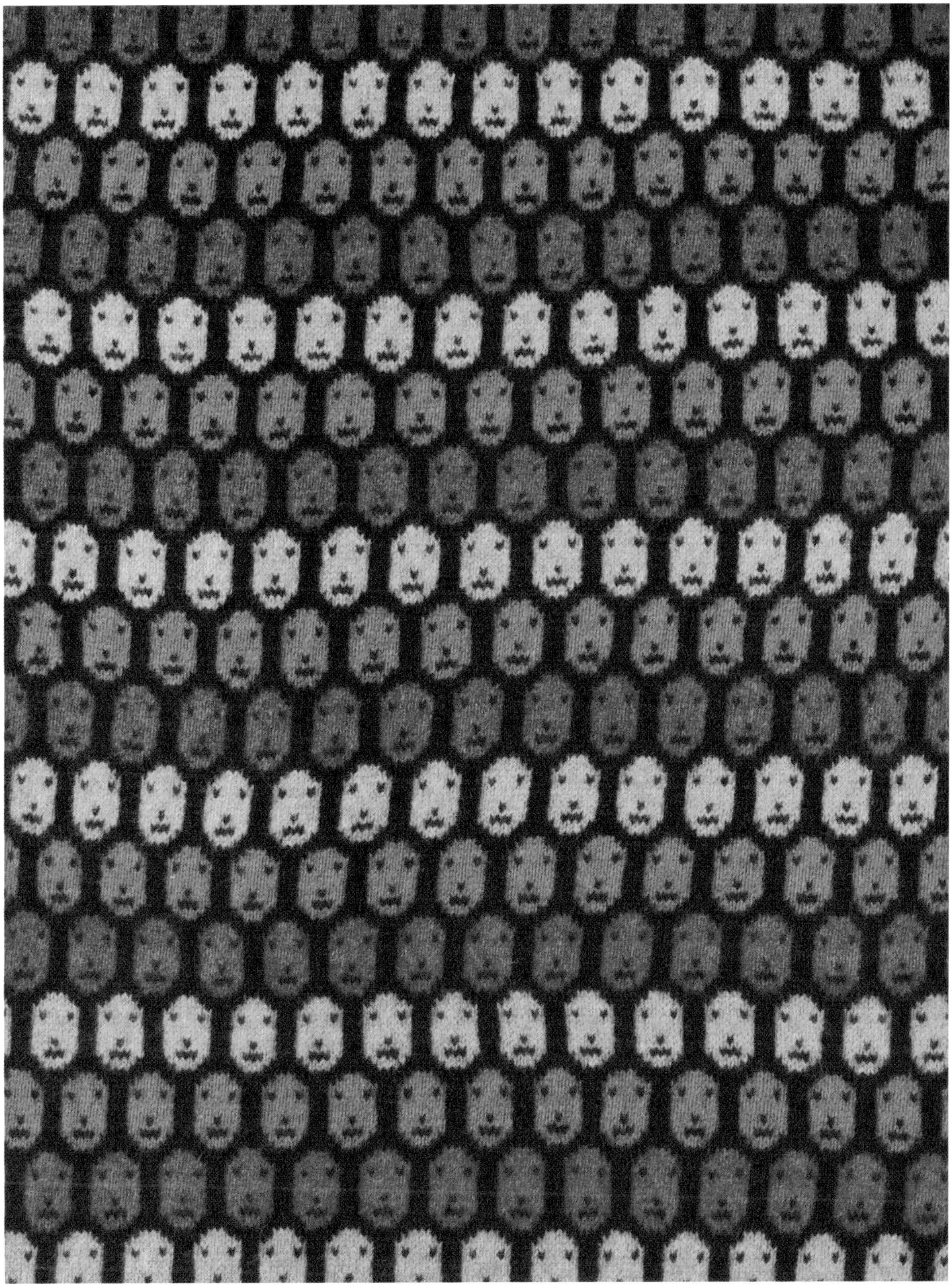

Mountain Spot — For SCP for range of woven kilim rugs.

マウンテンスポット — SPC のキリムラグに使用。

Fairisle — Designed for SCP for a range of rugs.

幾何学模様 — SCPのラグに使用。

Scope — Designed for SCP for a range of rugs.

スコープ — SCP のラグに使用。

# プロダクト・コレクション

# PRODUCT COLLECTION

ニットの人形

# CREATURES

Rudie Racoon
37cm

Rill
20cm

Wilbur
23cm

Bibi Bear
26cm

Ralf
20cm

Belle Bird
26cm

Peanut
29cm

Pablo
33cm

Pierre
39cm

Bruce
42cm

Smokey
26cm

Patch Cat
28cm

Ginge Cat
28cm

Mono cat
28cm

Shelly
41cm

Stick The Snail
24cm

Sidney
35cm

Mini Mushroom
Limited Edition
35cm

Suki Mushroom
33cm

Charlie Monkey
55cm

Jasper
38cm

Neep
38cm

Billy Broccoli
39cm

Mog Doll
(Green)
29cm

Cyril Squirrel Fox
37cm

Wolfie
31cm

Puddleman
43cm

Terry & Tina Twin
33cm

Peeping Tom
45cm

Molly
(Orange)
40cm

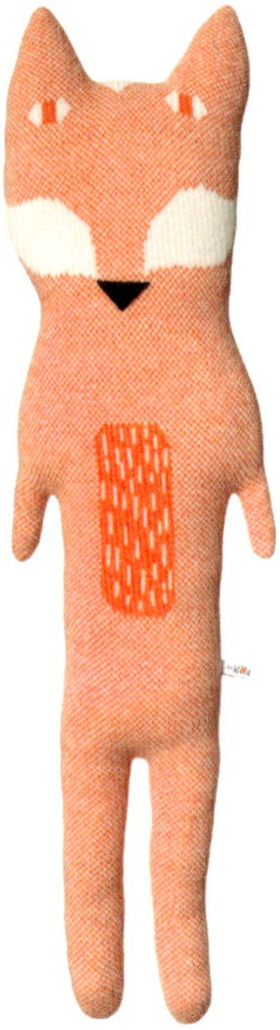

Angry Ginger
30cm

Stripy Head
(Blue)
25cm

Bunny Blue
23cm

Tig
15cm

Beryl dog
33cm

Big Fox
86cm

Big Ted
85cm

Berty
60cm

Rosie Mini
35cm

クッション

# CUSHIONS

Mountain Peek Cushion
(Bright Blue)
50 x 30cm

Mountain Peek Cushion
(Pastel)
50 x 30cm

Owl and Cat Round
Boat Cushion
(Navy)
46 x 36cm

Owl and Cat Round
Boat Cushion
(Oatmeal)
46 x 36cm

Owl and Cat Round
Boat Cushion
(Red)
46 x 36cm

Sea Boat Cushion
(Blue/Green)
50 x 30cm

Sea Boat Cushion
(Orange/White)
50 x 30cm

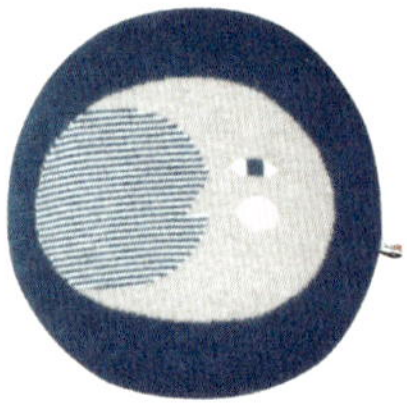

Cloud Lighting Cushion
60cm

Cloud Cushions from front
Pink-S 26cm
Grey-M 60cm
Blue-L 80cm
Grey-S 26cm

Cloud Rain Cushion
60cm

House Shaped Cushion
(Mustard)
48 x 40cm

House Shaped Cushion
(Pale Blue)
48 x 40cm

Sunshine Cushion Round
(Light Blue)
40 x 40cm

Moon Cushion Round
(Dark Blue)
40 x 40cm

Moon Cushion
(Blue/Yellow)
40 x 40cm

Sunshine Cushion
(Blue/Yellow)
40 x 40cm

Owl Cushion
(Mustard)
40 x 40cm

Robin Cushion
(Camel x Red)
40 x 40cm

Owl Cushion
(Green)
40 x 40cm

Robin Cushion
(Grey x Grey)
40 x 40cm

Bunny Cushion
(Grey)
40 x 40cm

Dog Cushion
(Jade)
40 x 40cm

Dog Cushion
(Red)
40 x 40cm

Fox Cushion
(Camel)
40 x 40cm

Fox Cushion
(Jade)
40 x 40cm

Badger Cushion
(Grey)
40 x 40cm

Badger Cushion
(Camel)
40x40cm

Badger Cushion
(Blue)
40x40cm

Badger Cushion
(Orange)
40x40cm

Leaves and Twigs
(Peacock)
44 x 44cm

Ogilvy
(Mushroom/Blue)
44 x 44cm

Meg
(Yellow)
44 x 44cm

Meg
(Orange)
44 x 44cm

Wolfie
(Mushroom/Grey)
44 x 44cm

Mog
(Grey/Pink)
44 x 44cm

Log Cabin Cushion
(Black x White)
48 x 48cm

Log Cabin Cushion
(White/Mustard)
48 x 48cm

Garden Cushion
(Natural)
60 x 60cm

Little Houses Cushion
(Camel)
40 x 40cm

Blah Blah Cushion
(Blue)
40 x 40cm

Blah Blah Cushion
(Pink x Red)
40 x 40cm

Small Faces Cushion
(Red)
40 x 40cm

Hofdi Cushion
(Oatmeal)
48 x 48cm

Playtime Cushion
(Primary)
48 x 48cm

Playtime Cushion
(Revel)
48 x 48cm

Town House Cushion
(Green)
24 x 35cm

Town House Cushion
(Oatmeal)
24 x 35cm

Town House Cushion
(Black/White)
24 x 35cm

Oak Leaf Tree
Large
55cm

Fir Tree
Small
28cm

Log Cushion
61 x 16cm

Tortoise Cushion
80cm

Small Twig Top Tree
180 x 21cm
Trunk 5cm

Rainbow Twig Smith Tree
225 x 21cm
Trunk 8cm

Minty Long Stalk
235 x 23cm
Trunk 6cm

Tall Peachy Petal Tree
170 x 20cm
Trunk 8cm

Pink Trunk Christmas Tree
120 x 40cm
Trunk 10cm

Pink Trunk Madge
145 × 30cm
Trunk 10cm

Pale Green Finger Tree
230 x 100cm
Trunk 19cm

Ziggy Pink Trunk
170 × 42cm
Trunk 15cm

ブランケット

BLANKETS

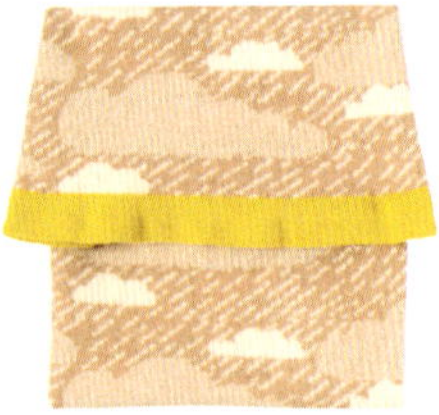

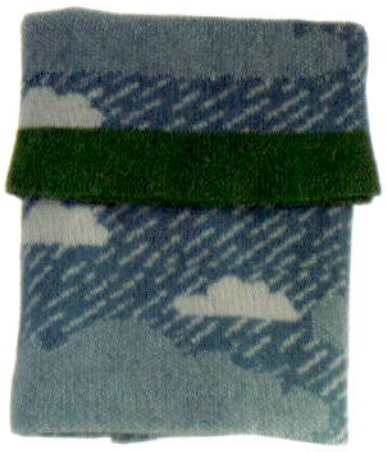

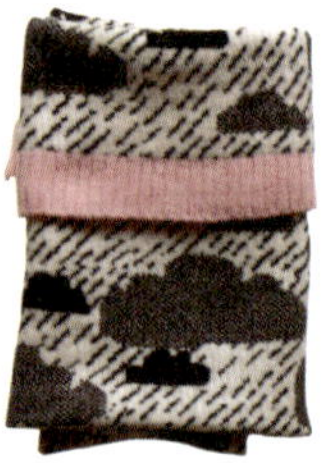

Rainy Day Mini Blanket
(Camel/Mustard)
95 x 62cm

Blah Blah Mini Blanket
(Blue)
95 x 62cm

Blah Blah Mini Blanket
(White/Black)
95 x 62cm

Mount Peak Cashmere
Mini Blanket
75 x 120cm

Rainy Day Mini Blanket
(Coral)
95 x 62cm

Rainy Day Mini Blanket
(Dark Blue)
95 x 62cm

Rainy Day Mini Blanket
(Blue/White)
95 x 62cm

Rainy Day Mini Blanket
(White/Ebony)
95 x 62cm

Boat Mini Blanket
(Pink/Orange)
72 x 70cm

Rainy Day Throw
(Pink)
190 x 145cm

House Throw
(Pink)
190 x 145cm

Boat Mini Blanket
(Blue/Green)
72 x 70cm

Rainy Day Throw
(Blue)
190 x 145cm

House Throw
(Green)
190 x 145cm

Boat Mini Blanket
(Orange/White)
72 x 70cm

Rainy Day Throw
(Grey)
190 x 145cm

Boat Mini Blanket
(Blue/Yellow)
72 x 70cm

House Throw
(Mustard)
190 x 145cm

House Blanket
(White/Pale Blue)
215 x 150cm

Woolywood Throw
(Brown)
190 x 145cm

Woolywood Throw
(Grey)
190 x 145cm

Blah Blah Throw
(White/Black)
190 x 145cm

Blah Blah Throw
(White/Pink)
190 x 145cm

Playtime
Mini Blanket
(Primary)
95 x 62cm

Playtime
Mini Blanket
(Green)
95 x 62cm

Mountain Peaks
Mini Blanket
(Pale Blue)
63 x 80cm

Mountain Peaks
Mini Blanket
(Bright)
63 x 80cm

Forest Floor Throw
(Black/White)
190 x 145cm

Forest Floor Throw
(Duck Egg/Green)
190 x 145cm

Nos Da Throw by Donna
Wilson for SCP
Top (Moss) / Middle (Blush)
/ Bottom (Mint)
180 x 150cm

## 帽子
## マフラー
## 手袋など

## HATS,
## SCARVES,
## GLOVES ETC

Circus Hat
(Blue/Orange)
One Size

Scandi Hat
(Grey)
One Size

Circus Hat
(White/Diesel)
One Size

Scandi Hat
(White)
One Size

Circus Hat
(Camel/Mustard)
One Size

Mountain Peak Hat
(Navy)
One Size

Dash Dot Hat
(Red/Beige)
One Size

Mountain Peak Hat
(Blue)
One Size

Tip Top Hat
(Gold/Blue)
One Size

Tip Top Hat
(Mint/Pink)
One Size

Circus Arm Warmers
(White/Diesel)
10 x 37cm

Circus Arm Warmers
(Blue/Orange)
10 x 37cm

Circus Arm Warmers
(Camel/Mustard)
10 x 37cm

Hofdi Scarf
(Magenta)
22 x 155cm

Hofdi Scarf
(Mustard)
22 x 155cm

Clyde Scarf
(Mustard/Caspian)
172 x 20cm

Clyde Scarf
(White/Tomato)
172 x 20cm

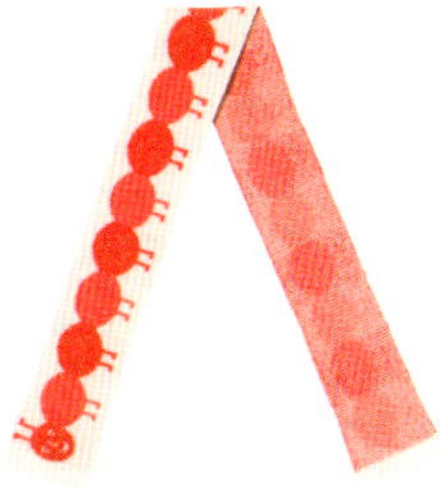

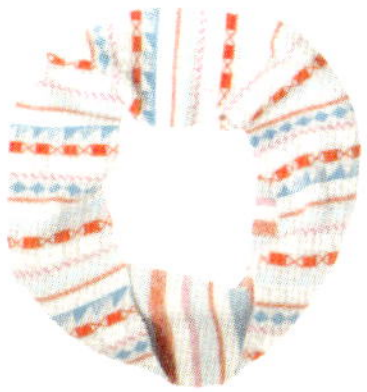

Caterpillar Scarf
(Grey/Blue)
116 x 10cm

Scandi Scarf
(Black)
One Size

Tutti Snood
(Orange/Black)
140 x 30cm

Caterpillar Scarf
(Blue/Green)
116 x 10cm

Scandi Scarf
(White)
One Size

Tutti Snood
(Grey)
140 x 30cm

Caterpillar Scarf
(Navy/Orange)
116 x 10cm

Graph Scarf
(Green)
160 x 24cm

Tutti Snood
(Pink)
140 x 30cm

Caterpillar Scarf
(Putty/Red)
116 x 10cm

Graph Scarf
(Orange/White)
160 x 24cm

Wooly Wood Snood
(Grey)
140 x 30cm

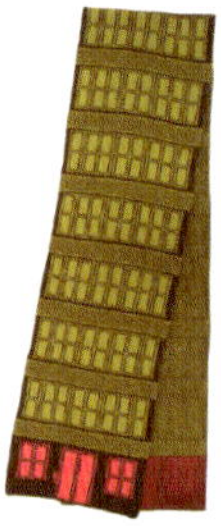

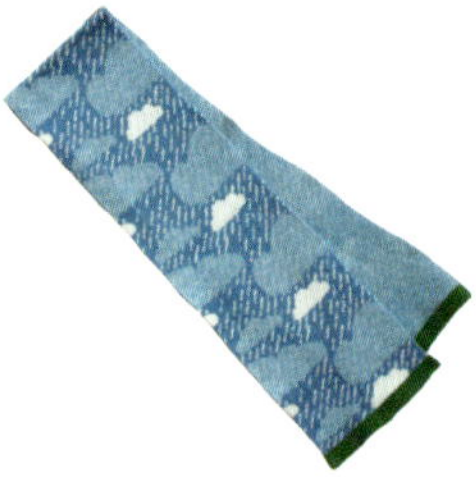

Skyscraper Scarf
(Grey/Pale Blue)
25 x 170cm

House Scarf
(Red/Beige)
28 x 152cm

Graph Scarf Wide
(Green)
160 x 24cm

Skyscraper Scarf
(Brown/Mustard)
25 x 170cm

Rainy Day Scarf
(White/Ebony)
19.5 x 150cm

Sausage Dog Scarf
(Blue)
14 x 150cm

House Scarf
(Black/White)
28 x 152cm

Rainy Day Scarf
(Blue/White)
19.5 x 150cm

Birdy Walk Scarf
(Green)
9 x 175cm

House Scarf
(Beige/Mustard)
28 x 152cm

Graph Scarf Wide
(Blue)
160 x 24cm

This Way Scarf
(Grey)
9 x 175cm

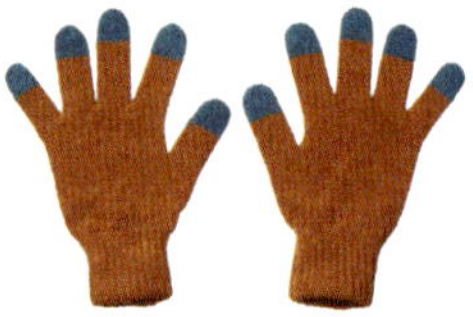

Fox Scarf
(Grey)
10 x 118cm

Fox Scarf
(Orange)
10 x 118cm

Bunny Scarf
(Grey)
10 x 145cm

Bunny Scarf
(Brown)
10 x 145cm

Swan Scarf (Big)
(Black)
7 x 174cm

Swan Scarf (Big)
(White)
7 x 174cm

Swan Scarf (Mini)
(Black)
4 x 97cm

Swan Scarf (Mini)
(White)
4 x 97cm

Flamingo Scarf
(Pink)
155cm

Tip Top Gloves
(Slate/Turquoise)
One Size

Tip Top Gloves
(Gold/Blue)
One Size

Tip Top Gloves
(Mint/Pink)
One size

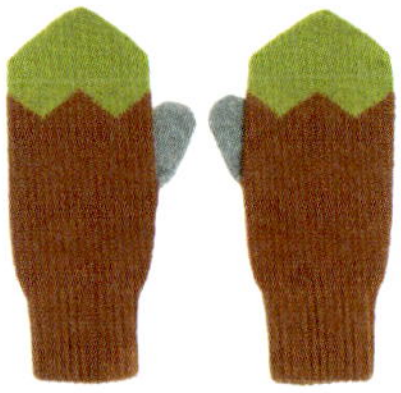
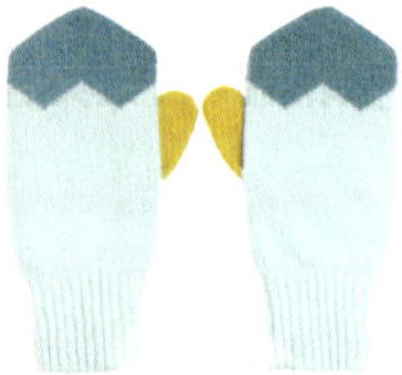

Graph Mittens
(Putty/Brown)
9 x 33cm

Graph Mittens
(Red/Green)
9 x 33cm

Dash Dot Pointy Mitt
(Green)
One size

Dash Dot Pointy Mitt
(Red/Beige)
One size

Zig Zag Mittens
(Green/Purple)
One Size

Zig Zag Mittens
(Olive/Brown)
One Size

Zig Zag Mittens
(Blue/Yellow)
One Size

Mountain Peak Mittens
(Navy)
One Size

Mountain Peak Mittens
(Grey)
One Size

Dash Dot Socks
(Beige/Mustard)
One Size

Graph Socks
(Orange/White)
One Size

Graph Socks
(Magenta)
One Size

陶器・ガラス

# CERAMICS, GLASSES

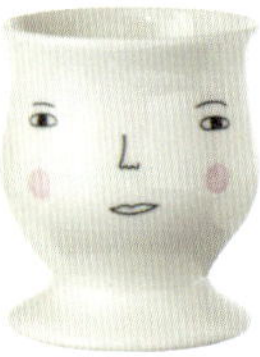

Hand-Painted
Staffordshire Dogs
(Sold in paires)
28 x 23cm wide each

Acorn Medium Bowl
5 x 15cmφ

Beardy Bob Egg Cup
6 x 5cmφ

Burt Egg Cup
6 x 5cmφ

Birdy Nest Egg Cup
6 x 5cmφ

Meg Egg Cup
6 x 5cmφ

Mog Egg Cup
6 x 5cmφ

Wolfie Beaker
10 x 7cmϕ

Owl Beaker
10 x 7cmϕ

Squirrel Beaker
10 x 7cmϕ

Grey Owl Beaker
10 x 7cmϕ

Bear Beaker
10 x 7cmϕ

Mog Plate
20cmϕ

Birdy Nest Plate
20cmϕ

Oak & Acorn Dinner Plate
27cmϕ

Acorn Plate
20cmϕ

Owl Plate
20cmϕ

Kaleidoscope Dinner Plate
27cmϕ

Birdy Walk Dinner Plate
27cmϕ

Meg Plate
20cmϕ

Grace Plate
20cmϕ

Beardy Bob Plate
20cmϕ

Fox Plate
20cmϕ

Baby Bear Small Bowl
H4cm x 13cmϕ

Mummy Bear Medium Bowl
H5cm x 15cmϕ

Daddy Bear Large Bowl
H6cm x 19cmϕ

Baby Plate
20cmϕ

On the Rocks Jug
20 x 11cmϕ

On the Rocks Tumbler
8 x 8cmϕ

Rock the Boat Tumbler
8 x 8cmϕ

Acorn Mug
H8.5cm x 8cmϕ

バッグ
ゆたんぽ

## BAGS,
## HOT WATER BOTTLES

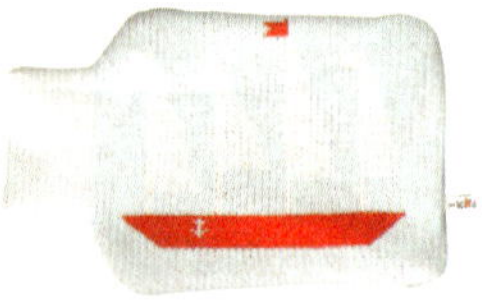

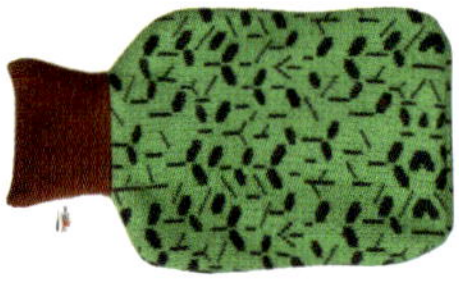

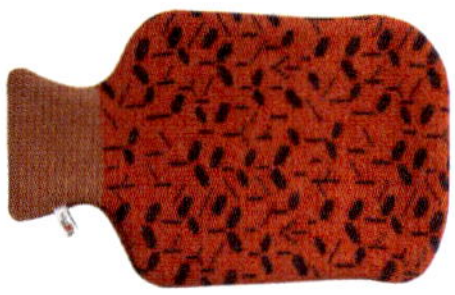

Beau Bag
(Brown)
15 x 12 x 9cm

Beau Bag
(Green)
15 x 12 x 9cm

Message In A Bottle
Hot Water Bottle
(Purple x Pink)
36 x 22cm

Message In A Bottle
Hot Water Bottle
(Pale Green/Blue)
36 x 22cm

Message In A Bottle
Hot Water Bottle
(Blue/Red)
36 x 22cm

Tree Hot Water Bottle
(Green/Brown)
38 x 23cm

Tree Hot Water Bottle
(Tiger)
38 x 23cm

Tree Hot Water Bottle
(Pale Green/Mustard)
38 x 23cm

家具

# FURNITURE

Ernest Pouffe in Nos Da by Donna Wilson for SCP (Blue Moon)
H30cm 60cmϕ

Henry Pouffe in Nos Da by Donna Wilson for SCP (Moss)
H45cm 45cmϕ

Albert Pouffe in Nos Da by Donna Wilson for SCP (Willow)
H7.5cm 70cmϕ

Ernest Pouffe in Braid by Donna Wilson for SCPCaspian (Caspian)
H30cm 60cmϕ

Henry Pouffe in Treecloud Blue by Donna Wilson for SCP (Treecloud)
H45cm 45cmϕ

Frank in Zig Zag by Donna Wilson for SCP (Red)
H40cm 80cmϕ

Bora Da Long Cusion by Donna Wilson for SCP (Willow)
W30 x L60cm

Molly Stool Low by Donna
Wilson for SCP
H33 x 30cmφ

Wilma Bench by Donna
Wilson for SCP.
W85 x D48 x H38cm

Eadie Armchair by Donna
Wison for SCP
W76 x H87 x D90cm

Bertha Armchair by Donna
Wilson for SCP
W82 x H83 x D83cm

Bertha Sofa by Donna
Wilson for SCP
W146 X D83 x H83cm

Wrapped Ercol Love Seat
W113 x H77 x D53cm

Wrapped Ercol Studio
Couch
W203 × H85 × D88cm

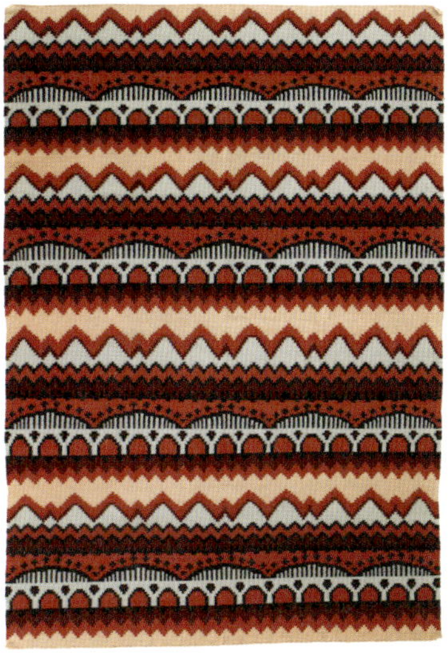

Bertha Cabinet by Donna
Wilson for SCP
W91 x H50 x D41cm

Fairisle Rug — Rose Cloud
by Donna Wilson for SCP
W140 x H200cm

Mountain Spot kilim —
Mustard Dust by Donna
Wilson for SCP
W120 x H180cm

Braid kilim — Papaya by
Donna Wilson for SCP
W120 x H180cm

# 発想のヒント

# INSPIRATION

## 風景

自然と触れ合うことが大好きです。子どもの頃は両親と農園に住んでいたので、よく外に散歩に出掛けました。空、草原、色彩や手触り、木、茂み、農作物。広々とした空間……そこに立つと私は生き生きできるんです。都会にいると、そういった自然が恋しくなります。最近はロンドンでも静かな地域に引っ越したので、新しい家には草木が茂る庭があります。もっと家で過ごす時間を増やすようにしたいです。

## THE LANDCSAPE

I love being outside in the countryside, and when I was young and lived with my parents on the farm, I'd go out for walks a lot. I love the sky, the fields, the colours and the textures, trees, bushes, and crops in the fields...the huge expanse of space... I can feel more alive. These things I really miss about the country, but we recently moved to a quieter part of London, and have a garden with grass and trees in it, so I hope I will feel more at home here.

雨

雨が嫌いな人も多いでしょう。でも、私とって雨は心地良いものなんです。それはもしかしたら、雨の日が多いことで知られるスコットランドで育ったからなのかも。窓や屋根に雨粒が落ちる時のぴちゃぴちゃという音を、家の中で聴いてるのが好き。レインコートにスカーフがあれば、外にいたって私は幸せです。雨に当たったからって怪我をする人はいないでしょう？「Puddleman」という人形は、水たまりでジャンプした思い出がもとになって誕生しました。

RAIN

Most people dislike the rain, but for me I find something quite comforting about it. It could be because my childhood was in Scotland where it has the reputation to rain a lot. I love the sound of the rain and the pitter patter on the window or roof when I'm nice and cosy inside. Or, if you are outside and all wrapped up in a coat and scarf, it makes me smile. Rain doesn't hurt! I made a creature called Puddle Man inspired by jumping in puddles.

秋

秋は私が一番好きな季節です。木の葉の色が変わって、寒くなってくれば、ウールのセーターを着られるから。それに、ちょうどその頃はクリスマスシーズンに向けて、たくさんの商品を作るためにスタジオが忙しくなります。それは私にとって大切な時期です。みんなで団結して、注文を受けた商品を世界中のお店やお客さんの元へ送り出します。なぜかそういった時のほうが私はリラックスしているから不思議。忙しくしているのが好きなんですね。クリスマスになれば、みんな２週間の休暇を取り、忙しかった分だけ楽しめます。

AUTUMN

Autumn is my favourite season. I love seeing the leaves changing colours, and it starts getting colder so I can wear my wooly jumpers again. Also for me, it normally marks the time when we get really busy in the studio and have to make lots and lots for our Christmas period. I like that time when everyone pulls together and we get all our orders out. It makes me relax more as I like being busy. Once it gets to Christmas, we all have two weeks off, and can really enjoy the holidays.

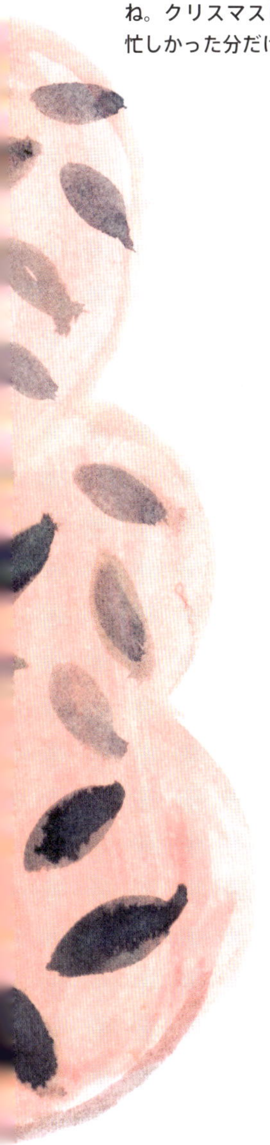

## 祖母

私が子ども時代を過ごしたのは、スコットランドの農園です。いつも絵を描いている子どもでした。私の祖母はバイタリティにあふれる人で、私と私の姉に絵を描くこと、ものごとを注意深く見ることの大切さを教えてくれました。彼女はちょっとしたアーティストで、私たちが描いた絵を額縁に入れて、近くの町のアートショーで売ったりしていました。そんな祖母の姿を見ていたので、自分の作品を売ってお金をいただけるということを、私は小さい頃から知っていたんです。

## MY GRANDMA

I grew up on a farm in Scotland and ever since I was child, I was always drawing and painting. I had a very inspiring grandmother who kept encouraging me and my sister to draw and look at things really closely. She was a bit of an amateur artist herself, so she would get our little doodles and drawings framed and then would sell them in local art shows in the nearest town. So from quite an early age I realized that you could sell your work and make money from it.

## 映画

映画は少しの間だけ、別の世界へ連れて行ってくれるから好きです。特に好きな作品は、ウェス・アンダーソンの『ザ・ロイヤル・テネンバウムズ』と『ライフ・アクアティック』。音楽、色合い、奇妙な人間関係、社会秩序を欠いた登場人物たち。それから、ミシェル・ゴンドリーの『恋愛睡眠のすすめ』も好きです。映画の中で登場人物が鍵盤を叩くとニットが編まれるピアノを発明するシーンは素敵。この映画には、ダンボールで作られたシーンがたくさん出てきます。これにインスピレーションを受けて、ダンボールのセットを背景に人形の写真を撮影したことがあります。

## FILMS

I love watching films, I think they can transport you into a different world for a while. I especially like Wes Andersons films like, ‘The Royal Tenebaums’ and ‘The Life Aquatic with Steve Zissou’. I love the music, the colour, the costumes and the strangeness of the relationships and dysfunctional characters. Another one of my favourite films is ‘The Science of Sleep’ by Michelle Gondry. There is a scene in it where the character invents a piano that knits when it is played! I found this film really inspiring as there were a number of scenes made entirely of card-board. This led me to making a card-board set for one of my photoshoots.

子どもたちの描く絵

いつも子どもが物事をどうやって見ているかに驚かされます。そこにはルールなんてありません。大きさ、奥行きは関係ないし、猫に足が５本もあったり、熊に大きな爪は付いてるのに足がなかったり！ 子供の頃の感性を、私も取り戻せたらと思っています。先入観を捨てて、制約されない想像力を使って創作してみたい。生まれたばかりの私の赤ちゃんは、もう絵を描き始めています。今は小さ過ぎるけど、あと何年かしたら、新しい人形のインスピレーションをもらえるはず！

CHILDREN'S DRAWINGS

I have always been inspired by how children see things...there are no rules. Scale and perspective are not important and it doesn't matter that a cat has 5 legs or a bear has huge claws but no legs. It's this innocence that I want to recreate in my work, forget about preconceptions, and just create using my uninhibited imagination! I'm really excited for my baby to start drawing. He is too young, but in a few years I might have more inspiration for new creatures!

## インスタレーション

人形を作るだけではなく、人形たちの住む世界を作るのも私の仕事です。それが実現できるのが、インスタレーション。ほぼ毎年一回はどこかのギャラリーで行っています。人形を等身大サイズに大きくしてみたり、１回だけのスペシャルアイテムを作ったりと、毎回さまざまな工夫を凝らしています。スペシャルアイテムは、その後に新しい商品として発売されることもあります。

## INSTALLATIONS

I wanted to make a world for my creatures to live in and doing installations in galleries has allowed me to do this. Nearly every year we have made an installation in a gallery space. It's been so much fun working to a bigger scale, and making one off special pieces. Sometimes this leads to new products too.

Me painting clouds at the Trico Gallery, Tokyo 2012.
2012 年、東京のトリコギャラリーで行なった展示で、窓ガラスに雲の絵を描きました。

Detail of nursery room at Somerset House 2013.
2013 年、サマーセットハウスの保育所の様子。

Detail shot of 'Escape to the Woods' show in the Lighthouse Gallery, Glasgow 2009.
2009年、グラスゴーのライトハウスギャラリーで行った展示「Escape to the Woods」。

Shot of all my creatures which inspired a small exhibition in Korea 2008.
2008年に韓国で行った展示からインスピレーションを得て撮影した人形の集合写真。

## ワークショップ

インスタレーションの他に、子どもから大人までいろいろな人に参加してもらうワークショップも行っています。「自分のモンスター人形を作ってみよう」といった、実際に参加者が手を動かしてニットを作る内容のワークショップがほとんどです。ルールに縛られないで、それぞれの想像力を生かしてもらいます。たとえば最近は、スコットランドのアバディーンシャーという町で、新しいタータン柄をデザインして欲しいという依頼を受けました。それに伴い、タータンのニットが作られる過程を地元の人たちと共有したくて、ワークショップも始めました。地元の子どもたちとのセッションでは「パンダの帽子を作ったことはある？」なんて可愛らしい質問をされたりするので、とても楽しい時間を過ごしています。

## WORKSHOPS

Besides installations, I have done a few workshops with kids and adults. Mainly it is for the paticipants to make things with their own hands, such as making your own monster workshops. I want to encourage people to use their imaginations and not stick to the rules there! Recently I have been asked to design a new tartan for Aberdeenshire. I've been working with the local community as I want everyone to feel involved in the process. It's been so much fun to go into schools as the kids ask the funniest questions like, "Have you ever made a panda hat?"

'Tartan Project', Aberdeenshire 2012/2014
2012、2014 年にアバディーンシャーで行った「タータンプロジェクト」。

2013年9月、ロンドンのICNギャラリーで行った、10周年記念パーティー。大きな人形は大好き。本当に彼らが存在していたら楽しいのに！会場ではフォトブースを設置して、来場者が巨大な人形と戯れている姿を撮影できるようにしました！

My 10 year anniversary show at the ICN Gallery, London, September 2013. I love the large creatures, and wish they would come to life! We set up a photo booth at the party and got lots of great photos of people having fun with the giants!

コラボレーション

コラボレーションはいつも新鮮な気持ちになれるから好きです。どんなものが出来上がるか想像できないところも魅力。自分自身に挑戦し続け、新しいものを生み出していくためには大切な作業です。家具のデザインを始めた頃はとても苦労しました。でも、ロンドンのインテリアショップ、SCP と密にやり取りしながら作業をすることで、とても素晴らしい作品を作り上げることができるようになりました。SCP はイギリス国内にインテリア装飾用品の工場を持っているので、私もその工場とあらゆることを相談しながら進めます。特に気に入っているのは、初めてデザインした「モトリー」というクッション付き長椅子。菱形のニットで構成されていて、チェスターフィールドのように留めてあります。これは、お互いの能力をバランスよく出し合った、完璧なコラボレーションでした！

COLLABORATIONS

I really enjoy collaborating with different people as it's a fresh way of working. You never know what might come out and it's great to keep challenging yourself and trying new things. The hardest thing for me to do was to start designing furniture, but I have worked so closely with SCP I feel we have done some really successful pieces. They have an upholstery factory in the UK which I collaborate with when we design a new piece together. One of my favourites is the first piece I designed for them, which is called 'Motley'. It's a large ottoman, with lots of knitted diamonds and buttoned like a chesterfield. I think it's a perfect collaboration, as it has an equal amount of me and SCP in it!

Left: 2010, Beautiful macarons for PIERRE HERMÉ PARIS in Japan, the made the most beautiful packaging from my watercolour drawings.

Right: 2011, Valentine special chocolate box, collaboration with a department store, ISETAN.

左：2010 年、日本で発売されたピエール・エルメ・パリのマカロン。私の水彩画をプリントした美しい箱を作ってもらいました。

右：2011 年、伊勢丹とのコラボレーションによるバレンタインチョコレート。

2007, 'Motley', frist collaboration with SCP.
2007年、SCPと完成させた「モトリー」。

2012, 'Henry pouffe', 'Frank pouffe' and 'Ernest pouffe' for SCP.
2012年、SCPとのコラボレーションで完成させた「ヘンリー・プーフ」「フランク・プーフ」「アーネスト・プーフ」。

2012, Collaboration with Rococo Chocolates, hand painted Easter eggs.
2012年、ロココ・チョコレートとのコラボレーションで作り上げた手描きのイースターエッグ。

2011, Wrapped Ercol 'Windsor Chair'.
2011年、毛糸を巻き付けたアーコール社の「ウィンザーチェア」。

SHOP LIST

AUSTRIA
Der Klein Salon
Le Shop

AUSTRALIA
KIDO Store
Made by Others
Miriam Bereson,
Opus Design Co.
Safari Living
Scout
Sedonia
SPACE
Third Drawer Down

BELGIUM
Au Detour Du Chemin
La Fabrika
Rewind
Sit on Design
Espoo

CANADA
Drake Hotel General Store
Galerie CO
Kit Interior Objects
MINT Interiors

CHINA
MOD Design Store

DENMARK
Area Store
HAY House

FRANCE
HOME Autour du Monde
Millimètres
Happy To See You
Les Enfants Du Design
Perlin Paon Paon

GERMANY
Blanket Store
Burger
Human Empire Shop
Luv Interior Hamburg
Perle-Shop
Pomeranza Design Ranch
Superjuju
Toendel

HONG KONG
Homeless
Mama Kid
Mushroom

ITALY
Yellow Basket
Nero

JAPAN
Trico International

THE NETHERLANDS
Wat Anders
Femkeido Shop
Buiten de Lijntjes
Depotrotterdam
Van Mij
Strand West
Tangram
Gosto
& Klevering Zuid
Imps & Elfs
Keet in Huis

NEW ZEALAND
Bob & Friends
Dunedin Public Art Gallery

NORWAY
Nest
ROST Oslo
ROST Bergen
Vitra Scandinavia Shop

PORTUGAL
Fabrica Features

SINGAPORE
The Little Drom Store

SLOVENIA
Sisi

SPAIN
Verdejade
Domestico Shop
Narata

SWEDEN
Malmo Modern
Mimmi Staaf Mobelmakeri

SWITZERLAND
Boutique Kitchener
MUDAC Shop
Einzigart

TAIWAN
Woow&Co

UK
John Lewis (Nationwide)
SCP East
SCP West
Liberty
Heals (Nationwide)
Smug
Cissy Wears
Southbank Centre Festival Terrace Shop
Future & Found
Indish
Three Potato Four
Soma Gallery
Yorkshire Sculpture Park
Frank
Dundee Contemporary Arts
Curiouser and Curiouser

USA
Entertaining Elephants
The Future Perfect
The Fabric Workshop and Museum
ABC Home Furnishings
Aldea Home
DownTown Knits
Kuhl-Linscomb
We are 1976
Woonwinkel
World of Mirth
ReForm School
Seattle Art Museum Shop

Trico International distributor
Canal court zone 3, 1-9-17-203
Shinonome Koto Tokyo 135-0062
JAPAN
Tel. + 81 3 3532 1901
www.bytrico.com

SCP East
135 Curtain Road
London EC2A 3BX
United Kingdom
Tel. +44 20 7739 1869
www.scp.co.uk

Official Website:
www.donnawilson.com

SPECIAL THANKS:

Everyone involved in this book — Åbäke Kajsa, Erika, Gareth Hacker, Natsumi, Kyoko.

Doing this book has made me look back on all the projects I have been involved in and the wonderful people I have worked with along the way.
I would like to say a special thanks to all my customers, some have collected my work, and supported me from the very beginning. Thank you, without you I wouldn't be able to make the things I make!

Also I want to mention Freddie Robins for being such a fantastic teacher and believing in me from the start. Sheridan Coakley, SCP for his fantastic support and challenging briefs, friendship and guidance.
My wonderful staff, past and present: Lousie Buchan, Erin McIntyre and Kate Beckett, and very talented team now — Rebecca Burns, Eva Joly, Laura Hwang, Sarah Milton, Ivonne, Holly and Cassie — it's been a pleasure working with everyone.

My wonderful family and of course Jon Almond, my partner who goes through all the stresses with me and always gives me his honest opnion! Thank you ALL!!

# ドナ・ウィルソン

スコットランドからやってきた、ニットの人形とテキスタイル

2013年12月10日　初版第1刷発行

著者　Donna Wilson
デザイン　Åbäke
写真　Gareth Hacker, Erika Wall, Donna Wilson
協力　SCP, Trico International
翻訳　藤田夏海
編集　藤田夏海，田本鏡子，石井早耶香

発行人　籔内康一

発行所　株式会社ビー・エヌ・エヌ新社
〒150-0022 東京都渋谷区恵比寿南一丁目20番6号
Fax. 03-5725-1511
E-mail. info@bnn.co.jp
www.bnn.co.jp

印刷・製本　シナノ印刷株式会社

ODD OBJECTS & TEXTILES

## DONNA WILSON

Published by BNN, Inc.

Author: Donna Wilson

Design by Åbäke, London with thanks to Mikako Umeda and Tomohiro Tsushi
Typeface: Donna, Axis Std R

Photo credits:

| | |
|---|---|
| Erika Wall | Cover, p.3, 6, 8-12, 46-77, 81 (Bottom), 85 (Top), 86, 88-95, 132-133, 191 |
| Gareth Hacker | p.17-43, 96-123, 135, 139, 141, 148-149, 150, 153, 157, 159, 161, 163, 187 |
| Donna Wilson | p.80, 81 (Top), 82-83, 172-171 |

Cooperation: SCP, Trico International
Thanks to: Derek Frampton Davis, Jodi Moss (SCP), Jonathan Ellery, Masashi Crete-Nishihata, Tomomi Kojo-Robertson, Yusuke Shouno

Translation: Natsumi Fujita
Edit: Natsumi Fujita, Kyoko Tamoto, Sayaka Ishii

Publisher: Kouichi Yabuuchi

Printing & Binding: SHINANO Co., Ltd.





ISBN978-4-86100-900-6



Printed in Japan